Nothing is wasted in the sanctifying wor' ...in our hearts. This is never more true th... ...life of motherhood. Using the wi... ...e-filled realities of the gos... ...s in all His glory as He tra... ...is are cleaning up spills, corralli... ...ided knees, the Lord is doing a good \ ...gh them—eternal work. Simona equips moms \ ...neir mothering and see the glorious wonder of Jesus Ch...ot.

Christina Fox,
Author of *Idols of a Mother's Heart*

'Where else can we go? You have the words of eternal life,' Peter told Jesus. Throughout this book Simona is reminding young mothers that the same principle is at work in their lives. There is nowhere else they can go for life but to Jesus. The simplicity and depth of the gospel ring out in this book as Simona meditates on words of eternal life and helps young moms apply them to their lives.

Gloria Furman,
Author of *A Tale of Two Kings* and *Labor with Hope*

Simona Gorton's book is a worthwhile read. The approach she uses to process the astonishing transition into motherhood and all that entails is valuable in several ways. Her method begins with Scripture, and we can observe and learn how to similarly sift our own experiences to sort the wheat from the chaff. Her conclusions are clear, and we can learn how to develop our own conclusions through prayer, study and meditation on God's Word, and careful gleaning from outside sources. Most importantly, she has captured the beauty of the power of the gospel of grace as we sift, sort, and work out lives of repentance and hope because of the glorious finished work of Christ.

KAREN GRANT,
Pastor's wife and co-founder, Franklin Classical Christian School, Franklin, Tennessee

What an encouragement Simona Gorton's winsome writing as a present day stay at home mom will be to her fellow laborers in this vital and often underappreciated calling. Using Ecclesiastes as a framework and pulling in lots of other pertinent Scripture, Simona carefully unpacks how the Lord can sanctify women to his glory as they faithfully serve him through their homes. Chock full of helpful quotes from Christians past and present, Simona's work will spur mothers on to joyfully embrace gospel truths as they swim against the culture and impact society one child at a time.

MARY K. MOHLER,
Director, Seminary Wives Institute, The Southern Baptist Theological Seminary, Louisville, Kentucky

Simona Gorton's account of biblical motherhood aims to draw our eyes up from the mundane (and chaotic!) in front of us to the unseen spiritual battle for our families, and the victory we already have in Christ. She assures us of the love and security we have in him, while encouraging us to constantly strive for growth in our mothering and in our own spiritual lives. In other words, this book is for mothers who are justified by Christ and longing to grow in sanctification. Simona is warm, funny, thoughtful, scriptural, and eminently relatable.

DAYSPRING MACLEOD,
Author, *10 Women Who Were Spiritual Mothers*

MOTHERING AGAINST FUTILITY

MOTHERING AGAINST FUTILITY

*Balancing Meaning and Mundanity
in the Fear of the Lord*

SIMONA GORTON

CHRISTIAN
FOCUS

Copyright © Simona Gorton 2025

Paperback ISBN: 978-1-5271-1187-5
Ebook ISBN: 978-1-5271-1260-5

10 9 8 7 6 5 4 3 2 1

First published in 2025
by
Christian Focus Publications Ltd,
Geanies House, Fearn, Ross-shire,
IV20 1TW, Great Britain

www.christianfocus.com

Designed and typeset by Pete Barnsley (CreativeHoot.com)

Printed by Bell & Bain, Glasgow

To my mother and mother-in-law

*Who forged first-generation faithfulness in their own
journeys of motherhood. Your examples have formed
the foundation for my mothering and—I pray—that
of generations to come.*

Contents

An Introduction

Then I saw that there is more gain in wisdom than in folly,
as there is more gain in light than in darkness.

ECCLESIASTES 2:13

The days after my first daughter was born were golden. I was still on maternity leave, and spring in Washington state was in full swing. In the Pacific Northwest we joke that we endure seven months of gray, rainy weather just for a few magical months of spring and summer. These blissful days were just beginning as April started off with young buds everywhere and I learned the ways of my newborn (as much as one can), planted a garden, and read.

As I started back at work part-time from home and my baby got older, dropped a few naps, and was joined by a baby sister, I started to feel stretched between the multiple callings in which I wanted to excel. Mothering, housekeeping, church investment, relationships, "wife-ing" and working all conspired to keep me just around a passing grade, and background guilt set in.

Is Everyone Pretending?

Somewhere along the line, guilt turned into resentment. How could *anyone* keep children relatively clothed and usually fed, clean the house with any level of consideration for sanitation standards (or even just out of desperation at the crumb count of the kitchen floor), hold down a job responsibly, and feel sane at all? I knew I was capable of great productivity, goal setting, and stellar time management. Yet here I was, barely keeping my head above water. It almost felt as if the entire thing had been rigged: if I couldn't do it, how could *anyone*? Was everyone who looked like they were doing it well just pretending?

That hot August, with a golden dog and two little girls (one of them just eight months old at the time and still very much breastfeeding), we moved across the country from Washington state to Pennsylvania and into an old farmhouse built in 1900 or before. It was a house that lacked upstairs air-conditioning and heat, but not character. Take, for instance, the bathroom with the gorgeous clawfoot tub but diarrhea-yellow wainscoting and faux-painted ceiling with gold borders and burnt ombre tones resembling an out-of-place Roman bathhouse. Or the oven which was proudly bought and installed when electric ovens first hit the American market (or thereabouts).

This move, the thick grime which coated everything, the piles of boxes in the basement to be unpacked, the crying baby who wanted to be nursed for the sixth time that day, and the fact that somehow by 2 p.m. nobody had magically prepared lunch, drove me to a new kind of desperation.

There may have been a meltdown or two, possibly some tears, while my gratitude deepened for a patient husband who didn't take to heart every word that passed through my lips.

But the utter insufficiency I felt during those days also drove me to Christ in a new way. I could hardly find enough minutes to finish the smallest task, much less keep my life together in the way I wanted, and I was becoming bitter about it. I knew I was deeply blessed in having a house, a husband, children of my own, and fulfilling work. Yet that somehow made it all worse and deepened the frustration and guilt I felt. I really should be able to do this. I could pretend for a few minutes. Maybe after the children were a bit older and not needing to be fed every two hours or spilling things or learning to squabble, I could pretend even better.

And yet I couldn't. I was falling flat on my face, desperate for any small feeling of accomplishment and control.

Naming Sin

Through the Spirit's conviction, I started to realize that this "tendency," this task-oriented "personality trait" was actually sin manifesting itself in my life. I was a naturally productive person when given an uninterrupted hour and a Billy Joel playlist, but throw in a dropped bowl of oatmeal, a fussy infant, and a taped-off room that had stared me in the face for two weeks asking to be painted, and I felt like a caged animal. I might have acted a bit like one too. I lived like this was *my* life, *my* time, *my* endless, essential task list, and how *dare* anyone stand in *my* way?!

My drive to accomplish things, while it could move mountains, had become an idol of the heart for control and productivity, and it was damaging the fabric of my home. It was sucking the joy out of my toddler begging me, "Pwease can we read a book, Mommy!" It was building stress in me as I walked from room to room of this beautiful old home, frantically tidying up and annoyed that my husband wasn't a project-doing, picture-hanging, floor-restoring robot. It had me mentally rehearsing the list of undone and previously-unthought-of-but-now-immediately-pressing tasks as I fell into bed, exhausted to my core.

In retrospect, God was robbing me of my idol of productivity to show me more of Himself. He was bringing me face to face with my own insufficiency so that He could fill me with His strength and reformat my identity. I needed to recognize that I had been working for my own sanity and sense of satisfaction and not primarily for *Him*. I was constantly working to get that "high" from getting things done, rather than sating my soul in Christ and finding my satisfaction in Him. He had not created me primarily to work, but to bring glory to His name and to highlight His worthiness. The difference was becoming painfully apparent.

The stark, biblical naming of this sin in my heart was deeply convicting, but also freeing. It unbound me from a string of similar sins going back years. These failures were all covered in the blood of Christ and they did not define me. At the same time, they unearthed the roots of a sin that had grown down deep and twined themselves around my heart. Digging it out would need some serious attention. This began my journey to pursue "the good portion"[1]: of understanding what it meant to submit truly to the work of each day to Jesus and see it as worship of *Him* and not as worship of *me* (albeit subtly re-cast to be more respectable).

---

1   *Everyday Worship* by Trisha Wilkerson (Christian Focus, 2013) explores the story of Mary and Martha to examine this biblical theme more deeply.

About the same time, I started to realize how the book of Ecclesiastes spoke specifically to many of my challenges as a mother. How could the multitude of inconsequential dishes and diapers and dinners that crowded my days feel so trivial but also hold so much real meaning as the building blocks of a life to which God had called me? How could my days as a mother, made up of "nothings" like going to the library and wiping small popsicle faces be the instruments of God's eternal plan through generations? Ecclesiastes had an answer to this tension, and I started to meditate on the truths of this book as they applied to the days and to-do lists I was learning to submit to the Lord.

Daily Vanity

The book you're holding isn't meant to be a commentary on Ecclesiastes, or even exclusively about Ecclesiastes. Rather, specific themes from the book, seen in light of the glorious gospel of redemption, will help form a framework through which we can view our calling as mothers.

Ecclesiastes has something to say to us mothers. As we face the "vanity" of menial work every day, we have the privilege of learning to not only see through it to greater realities but to see the tasks themselves as accomplishing something of lasting value in us and in those around us. In the calling of motherhood, God transforms our sight and opens our eyes to the gospel dichotomies of weakness as strength, smallness as glory, inefficiency as faithfulness. Our lives and actions as mothers, surrendered to Him like loaves and fishes, can become stunning showpieces of gospel hope, glimpses of eternal hilarity and joy.

As you will hopefully see very clearly, I do *not* have it all together and anything of worth you find in these pages is a grace passing from Jesus through me, in all my daily failings, to you. I am not writing this book "to you"—it's really "with you," in the sense that I'm drafting it in between putting the baby down for a nap, and giving the older child a pen and hoping she draws in the coloring book and not in some other creative place, and walking up and down stairs that haven't been vacuumed in. . . well now, we may be getting off topic.

This book is coming to you from the front lines of my home and I'm studying these things as much for the enrichment of my own heart as for the goal of encouraging you in your own day-to-day mothering. My experience of these truths is not terribly remarkable or heroic and I am likely only putting words to things you have already indescribably felt and thought as you walked through your own pathways of mothering.

Lastly, I would encourage you to find an older woman, or several, from your local church who can offer timely, in-person counsel. Older members of our churches are those whom the Lord has placed in our lives to share their own experiences and wisdom gleaned from years of reading the Word and seeing it transform them and their own mothering. Find a woman who radiates Christ and treasures her Bible, then invite her to know you, to speak into your life, and to give you a pattern to follow as you seek to faithfully serve Christ.

I pray that you, my friend, might glean something of value as you read this little book and become increasingly equipped for the responsibilities of your days and the training of young warriors for the King. May our Jesus ever get all the glory for Himself.

Experience and Ecclesiastes

*And whatever my eyes desired I did not keep from them.
I kept my heart from no pleasure, for my heart found
pleasure in all my toil, and this was my reward for all my
toil. Then I considered all that my hands had done and the
toil I had expended in doing it, and behold, all was vanity
and a striving after wind, and there was nothing to be
gained under the sun.*

ECCLESIASTES 2:10-11

Do you remember hearing as a newly pregnant mom about the exhaustion that comes with that first baby? How tired you would be? You thought, "*Yeah, yeah, I know what I'm signing up for.*" At least I thought *I* did.

Then the baby arrived and somewhere about forty-eight hours afterwards my eyes started to feel like they had gravel in them. My two-hour alarm—set when I *began* feeding, not *ended* it—was most certainly heartless and my blanket became lead itself whenever that same alarm went off (just thirty seconds after my head hit the pillow). Not to mention the unspeakable soreness and pain of recovery and nursing.

All of a sudden I realized in my bones the sort of tiredness that all other mothers since time began had experienced and what my own mother likely went through with me. And it became *real*. I didn't know exactly how true all the warnings of mothers were until I myself became one, in all my leaky, sore, tired splendor. I suddenly wanted to hug every passing mother and tell her she was a hero. And maybe I secretly wanted someone else to tell me that *I* was a hero. I did once actually have a stranger at the grocery store graciously allow me to take her place in line, saying, "Mothers are the heroes of the world"—she had no idea how much her encouragement meant that day.

This is the kind of wisdom Ecclesiastes teaches—the *learned* kind, not just the memorized information kind. The writer actually searched out and pursued meaning and fulfillment. He didn't just sit around thinking about them and writing down his theoretical thoughts. Think of it as the difference between a verified autobiography and a novel. What Solomon learned isn't just worth listening to because it sounds good but because it is the omniscient God teaching us from His stores of wisdom and doing it through the actual experience of a man who breathed the same air as we do.

Living Wisdom

First and foremost, then, Ecclesiastes is worthy of our attention because it is the living and active Word of God, able to pierce our hearts and change our understanding. Through the Spirit's power, it daily transforms us, turning us away from useless things and giving us life in the way of the Lord (Ps.119:37).

But in His mercy and condescension, the Lord has chosen to give this wisdom to us in the form of the actual experience of a flesh and blood man who has walked the path of life on planet earth. Its principles ring truer to our ears the further along the path of life we walk. As 1 Corinthians 10:13 says, "No temptation has overtaken you that is not common to man. God is faithful, and he will not let you be tempted beyond your ability, but with the temptation he will also provide the way of escape, that you may be able to endure it."

God has done one better than the writer of Ecclesiastes. The Son of God Himself came to earth to walk for thirty years in our shoes. He faced distractions, temptations, betrayal, disease—and through it all, He kept His eyes on the Father. He worked as a carpenter, chiseling, cutting, and sanding actual wood, cleaning up actual sawdust, working with customers, interacting with sinful siblings and parents, then waking up and doing it all over again. Hebrews 4:15-16 says,

> For we do not have a high priest who is unable to sympathize with our weaknesses, but one who in every respect has been tempted as we are, yet without sin. Let us then with confidence draw near to the throne of grace, that we may receive mercy and find grace to help in time of need.

He knows all about the stage setting of Ecclesiastes and of our own lives. In fact, He designed the original, perfect set, before we came through with a sledgehammer and ruined most of it. But He came to live in the desecrated set with us not only to redeem us, but to show us how to really and truly *live*.

Like the writer of Ecclesiastes, Jesus faced the dichotomy of life in this straining, pre-eternity world: the same dichotomy we face every day. But unlike the writer of Ecclesiastes, He didn't have to try out all the ways of finding real joy. He *knew* the only way to true joy, and He lived it out in front of us. He lived out what it means to fully delight in God while being faithful in the vanity that is this world. He lived out what it means to obey and find real satisfaction in that obedience even when it didn't make sense to those around Him.

Jesus lived out obedience to the fullest, and He died in obedience so that the power of death might be broken and we might once again have the power to resist sin. He obeyed, living to the glory of His Father alone and dying to redeem us. As the writer of Hebrews put it a few chapters earlier, "Since therefore the children share in flesh and blood, he himself likewise partook of the same things, that through death he might destroy the one who has the power of death, that is, the devil (Heb. 2:14)."

As redeemed believers, we walk in the power of the Spirit, able once again to disobey the inclinations of our flesh and the promptings of our sinful heart and to walk in the way of obedience to God and His commands.

Following Jesus' example, the fear of the Lord guides us as we walk on this earth, giving us the starting point and foundation for wisdom in a complicated, confusing, broken world. As Proverbs 9:10 explains, "The fear of the LORD is the beginning of wisdom, and the knowledge of the Holy One is insight." Apart from this fear, we are truly adrift (whether we recognize it or not).

As Michael Reeves observes rightly in his excellent book *Rejoice and Tremble*, "The fear of the Lord is the only fear that *imparts* strength. This is an especially vital truth for any who are called to some form of leadership (like mothers), for the strength this fear gives is—uniquely—a *humble* strength. Those who fear God are simultaneously humbled *and* strengthened before his beauty and magnificence."[2] This fear is not a cowering fear, but a rightly-ordered response of love to the revelation of an eternal, all-powerful Deity. There is truly no way to live rightly in the world God has made apart from this fear of God.

Vanity: Which Kind?

But let's back up a little. We've started talking about the word "vanity" but that may be bringing up images of Shirley Temple staring in a mirror and stroking her permed headful of golden curls while murmuring, "Aren't I pretty?" This kind of vanity is more tangible, perhaps, than the other kind of vanity we often can't quite put our finger on—the kind that means something is a bit useless, without real value.

One of the best dictionaries in the English language, Webster's 1828, lists out the following definitions of the word "vanity":

1. Emptiness; want of substance to satisfy desire; uncertainty; inanity.

2. Fruitless desire or endeavor.

3. Trifling labor that produces no good.

4. Emptiness; untruth

5. Empty pleasure; vain pursuit; idle show; unsubstantial enjoyment.

6. Ostentation; arrogance.

---

2   Michael Reeves, *Rejoice and Tremble* (Wheaton: Crossway, 2021), Everand.

7. Inflation of mind upon slight grounds; empty pride, inspired by an overweening conceit of one's personal attainments or decorations...

"Empty," "fruitless," "trifling," "idle," "unsubstantial." All these words capture aspects of the vain existence about which the writer of Ecclesiastes set out to know more. For a thing to be "vain" doesn't mean it is necessarily evil, but simply that in itself it has no lasting value, no eternal worth. This is why we see Solomon coming up dry again and again to say, "This also is vanity and a striving after wind."

Our lives, particularly as mothers, seem to be made up almost entirely of "vain" things as we wash dishes and change diapers and sweep floors and wipe up puddles of water (we hope) in the bathroom all day long. What more appropriate example of "striving after wind" than a mother keeping her floors clean? This is exactly the reason we of all people need anchors of deep, lasting hope as we walk through our days (Heb. 6:18-19). We need the anchor to hold while we ride the waves of each day of mothering small people and seek wisdom to live out eternal hope before their eyes.

So what does it mean to submit all the "vanity" of life— the things that seem at best like drudgery and at worst like a waste—to the Lord, trusting that in His hands, all these trivialities are being redeemed for eternity?

The answer is Christ.

Great. Perfect Sunday school answer. But how does the reality of Jesus and His life and death and resurrection change a morning going wrong already by 6 a.m.? I know He has given me this important work of raising children, but how does that help me cheerfully greet these actual children when they wake up an hour early and obliterate my morning quiet time?

We all know that taking simple biblical principles and applying them to our real lives is rarely a simple matter, which is why I wrote this book . . . and why you're holding it.

Applying Ecclesiastes to Motherhood

In the pages ahead, we'll explore this dichotomy practically on a number of levels because it is here that the vanity and toil and sweat of Ecclesiastes, in all their insignificant earthiness, meet the eternal purposes of God to redeem a people for Himself and to bring them home to glory. Stubborn children and dirty kitchen floors and everything in between are revealed to be the essential heavenward manuals that they were designed to be.

The old hymn, "Turn Your Eyes Upon Jesus", describes the solution more vibrantly than I ever could:

> *O soul are you weary and troubled*
> *No light in the darkness you see*
> *There's light for a look at the Savior*
> *And life more abundant and free.*

> *Turn your eyes upon Jesus*
> *Look full in his wonderful face*
> *And the things of earth will grow strangely dim*
> *In the light of his glory and grace.*

> *His word shall not fail you he promised*
> *Believe him and all will be well*
> *Then go to a world that is dying*
> *His perfect salvation to tell.*

It's only in looking to Jesus that the distractions and troubles, and even the joys of this world, will be put in their proper perspective. We are actors in this drama of life, not victims, and it is the God who, in Christ, made Himself the real victim of our sin and world-shriveling death that makes our sight clear.

3

All Is Vanity—or Is It?

The words of the Preacher,
the son of David, king in Jerusalem.
Vanity of vanities, says the Preacher,
Vanity of vanities! All is vanity
What does man gain by all the toil
at which he toils under the sun?

…

All streams run to the sea, but the sea is not full;
To the place where the streams flow,
There they flow again.

ECCLESIASTES 1:1-3, 7

Have you ever walked downstairs in the early morning before it's entirely light out, expectant for a new day and determined for a new start, only to see the sink full of dishes and remember the foolhardy decision to party with your husband last night and leave the dishes for later? Now they're all eyeing you with the encouraging reminder that they'll need to be cleaned or shoved aside to make breakfast in a few minutes for hungry little mouths. Just me?

You scoot aside the mostly-eaten remains of dinners on sticky counters, knowing that after these are cleaned, there will somehow magically be just as many dishes that appear again before lunchtime even begins. Oh, and the dishwasher just broke.

Nagging in the back of your head is the thought, *Why even try? What is this all going to?* The hamster wheel of household responsibilities can threaten to take over our thoughts and emotions and make us forget the goal of all our labors under the sun. Like the singer and songwriter Rich Mullins put it so aptly,

> *Sometimes the morning came too soon*
> *Sometimes the day could be so hot*
> *There was so much work left to do*
> *But so much you'd already done.*[3]

Yes, yes, I think. *I grew up memorizing the catechism and I* know *my chief end is to "glorify God and to enjoy Him forever."* It's just that my chief end seems to get lost somewhere in between continuous loads of laundry and that fleeting sense of accomplishment when the floor is finally swept *and* mopped one day out of the month.

Somewhere in all this is the true meaning of my existence, but, as I fight to keep my eyes on that rather than on all the chaos, I become more and more convinced that the mundanity itself is a signpost pointing us to the glory of God if we'll let it. The very vanity of this life is meant to help us live out our chief

---

3   Rich Mullins, "Sometimes by Step," n.d., track 3 on *Songs*, 1986, Reunion Records, Inc., Spotify.

end and it becomes the vehicle enabling us to fulfill it in this life before we perfectly fulfill it one day in glory.

The Pitfall of the Ethereal: Gospel without Ecclesiastes

One of the mercies of this sometimes-too-tangible calling right in front of us is that it actually helps us avoid being "so heavenly minded we're not of any earthly good." We don't often have the liberty of long quiet times with a hot cup of tea and freshly buttered toast. We're more often grabbing quick sips of cold coffee between buttering toast for a tearful toddler and rescuing someone else from playing in the trash (or better yet, the toilet). We work to get a few minutes of soul-food in the Word before the house wakes up because we know we need it to survive the day and we work to remember these snippets of truth and overarching reality. The truths we read often get applied right away and sink down more deeply than they did when we had more time to ourselves.

Our callings as mothers rescue us from having our heads in the clouds and going through life thinking that insightful Bible study time equals growth in sanctification. Don't get me wrong—the hardship of motherhood doesn't itself sanctify us, only the blood of Christ. We must daily work to feed our souls on the steadying truth of the Word. Yet motherhood is like a program custom-designed by God to rescue us from our own myopia. It has a way of clearing away the fog of self-deception we so often carry around with us and helping us learn the same lessons about ourselves and about the mercy of God over and over in ever deepening ways that evidence themselves in the dust and grit of the road we're walking.

We all know it deep down: if we don't manifest the gospel here in our homes, where "nobody" is watching, we're pretty much fakes. We cannot be godly Christians who serve faithfully at church but neglect the hearts of our children and snap selfishly at our husbands.

Of course, we all have different strengths and skill sets, and the Lord presses in on each of us in different areas in specific seasons of our lives. But the real truth about who we are and who the Lord is making us to be as imitators of His Son can be most clearly seen within the walls of our home. Elisabeth Elliot wrote, "The process of shaping the child…shapes also the mother herself. Reverence for her sacred burden calls her to all that is pure and good, that she may teach primarily by her own humble, daily example."[4]

The Pitfall of Despondency: Ecclesiastes without Gospel

This leads us to one of the conundrums of Ecclesiastes. Solomon was the wisest man who ever lived, but it seems he had to experiment with all the ways to be fulfilled before discovering the only true way (or being reminded of it). His father, David, had written, "Turn my eyes from looking at worthless things and give me life in your ways"[5] but his son, it seems, dove headfirst into all kinds of worthless things before discovering life in God.

"And I applied my heart to seek and to search out by wisdom all that is done under heaven," wrote Solomon. "It is an unhappy business that God has given to the children of man

---

4   Elisabeth Elliot, *The Shaping of a Christian Family* (Grand Rapids: Revell, 2021), Everand.

5   Ps. 119:37.

to be busy with. I have seen everything that is done under the sun, and behold, all is vanity and a striving after wind. What is crooked cannot be made straight, and what is lacking cannot be counted." (Eccl. 1:13–15)

Sounds hopeless, doesn't it? Almost depressed. One thing is for sure: it wouldn't have done him too much harm to read through his father's own book of Psalms to refocus his sight on the particular day he wrote this.

Yet somehow, we also feel the rightness in Solomon's sober-minded approach as he works through the realities of life in the pages of Ecclesiastes:

> Rejoice, O young man, in your youth, and let your heart cheer you in the days of your youth. Walk in the ways of your heart and the sight of your eyes. But know that for all these things God will bring you into judgment.
> — Ecclesiastes 11:9

Egged on by the world and all its cares and distractions, we subconsciously insulate ourselves from the contrast between earthly fluff and eternal weight. There is something refreshing about the facts being laid bluntly before us.

> Again I saw that under the sun the race is not to the swift, nor the battle to the strong, nor bread to the wise, nor riches to the intelligent, nor favor to those with knowledge, but time and chance happen to them all. For man does not know his time.
> — Ecclesiastes 9:11-12

Deep down we know these things are true: that judgment is coming to all; that nobody knows the path their life will take; that unexpected tragedies happen to both good people and bad people; that success in life isn't dictated by how much we pour into it; in short, that the ultimate ordering of things isn't in our power to control. No matter how much we believe the truth of the gospel, we are often nagged by the futility of our efforts to "do what we're supposed to" or to "be good people."

Isn't this struggle at the heart of our lives as mothers? We wonder sometimes what God is possibly doing through all our mundane counter messes and bedraggled rainy school days. How can it all possibly matter for eternity? How do we hold real, solid gospel hope in the forefront of our minds while we're wading through feelings of futility?

We need the truth of the gospel close beside us along this path. Not as an imponderable manual written in seven languages, but as a friend to come alongside us and embrace us in our weakness and forgetfulness. Those of us who believe the gospel still struggle to look to Christ for our fulfillment and meaning. We distract ourselves with social media when our lives don't look the way we think they should; we grumble to our husband when our children don't behave the way they ought; we think longingly of the lifestyle we wish we had (or that we gave up to have children); we run from Christ when we fail instead of running to the One who has open arms for us even—especially—when we fail and falter.

This is why we need to be reminded over and over and over again that God cannot be surprised by our sin, and that His grace is more determined to transform us than we are determined to resist that transformation. As the heartening lyrics to "His Mercy is More" by Matt Boswell and Matt Papa rejoice,

What love could remember no wrongs we have done
Omniscient, all knowing, He counts not their sum
Thrown into a sea without bottom or shore
Our sins they are many, His mercy is more.

What patience would wait as we constantly roam
What Father, so tender, is calling us home
He welcomes the weakest, the vilest, the poor
Our sins they are many, His mercy is more.[6]

We need the gospel to breathe life into the earthbound realities of Ecclesiastes in our days. Without the truths of Ecclesiastes, the good news of the gospel can float a few inches above ground level where the months of dust have accumulated in the corners of our living room. Yet without the gospel, Ecclesiastes can bring down the heart in despondency and the hopeless fragility of living in a sin-sick world. We need both in our pilgrimage on this earth.

Bridging the Gap

Charles Bridges, in the preface to his commentary on Ecclesiastes, quoted John Cotton, "What a stimulus to seek after the true and full knowledge of Christ is the realized conviction of the utter vanity of all things else without Him."[7]

Solomon lived in hope of a coming Christ, yet knew little of Him and the redemption He would bring. We must take his Spirit-inspired wisdom for life in a fallen world into our days with the now-known hope of Christ's coming to earth

---

6   Matt Boswell and Matt Papa, "His Mercy is More," n.d., track 1 on *His Mercy is More*, 2019, Getty Music Label, Spotify.

7   Charles Bridges, *Ecclesiastes* (Edinburgh: Banner of Truth Trust, 2021), vii.

and hold both in tension from the moment of our waking until the moment our head hits the pillow (and every time it rises in the night).

The good news of God saving sinners through the righteousness of His Son and preserving them through their entire lives to be resurrected in glory one day and to live with Him forever is enough to fill our hearts and souls with joy. Yet often we would rather work hard and have the sense of at least partially earning the same grace Christ is waiting to simply bestow on those who know they could never earn it.

Dane Ortlund, in his excellent book on the Gospels, describes how counterintuitive Christ's message was to the "good," law-abiding Pharisees (and we all have more in common with them than we'd like to admit). He writes, "[The] point is that, in the kingdom of God, the one thing that qualifies you is knowing that you don't qualify, and the one thing that disqualifies you is thinking that you do."[8]

Not only is Christ the wellspring of all meaning in this world, but He gives purpose to even the mundanity of our lives and is gentle with us in our straining and striving. He holds out to us the joys of eternal life, free for the taking. He is merciful to those who know their own need and who come to Him for grace in their weakness and sin for grace. David exults in Psalm 34,

> I sought the LORD, and he answered me
>> And delivered me from all my fears.
> Those who look to him are radiant,
>> And their faces shall never be ashamed.

---

8   Dane Ortlund, *Surprised by Jesus* (Leland: Evangelical Press, 2021), p. 45.

This poor man cried, and the LORD heard him
    And saved him out of all his troubles.
…
The LORD redeems the life of his servants;
    None of those who take refuge in him
    will be condemned.
— Psalm 34:4-6, 22

4

Remembering the Goal

He has made everything beautiful in its time. Also, he has put eternity into man's heart, yet so that he cannot find out what God has done from the beginning to the end…I perceived that whatever God does endures forever; nothing can be added to it, nor anything taken from it. God has done it, so that people fear before him. That which is, already has been; that which is to be, already has been; and God seeks what has been driven away.

ECCLESIASTES 3:11, 14-15

Some Sunday mornings the baby naps and I shower, put my makeup on, blow-dry my hair, and get dressed all in one blissful, uninterrupted sequence, punctuated only by my daughter running in from the kitchen to show me balloon animals her daddy is making her. Balloon rams, if you must know, apparently have oversized horns and under-developed hindquarters. These are a rare breed, along with the Sundays which I have just described.

Other Sundays, the disorder of the house is causing my stress level (read "ungodly anxiety") to rise, and I peevishly feel that I am doing *much* more than my fair share to get the family out the door and someone (not me) peed their pants at the least opportune time and we're magically late (again) despite our best efforts, and most of the drive to church is spent discussing why the subtle "I need your help" signals were not read flawlessly by my husband and how that is the whole reason our family is not driving to church in a sanctified state.

Meanwhile, internally, I know I've acted selfishly and been short with the peeing toddler and ungracious to my husband and I guiltily stumble through the doors of the church *knowing* I'm a sinner in desperate need of grace. The reality is, I'm just as much a sinner in desperate need of grace on the animal balloon Sundays, but I remember it better on the hard Sundays.

Transformation for Eternity

In Philippians 2:12-13, Paul writes,

> Therefore, my beloved, as you have always obeyed, so now, not only as in my presence but much more in my absence, work out your own salvation with fear and trembling, for it is God who works in you, both to will and to work for his good pleasure.

So much is packed into these verses. The first thing I tend to notice is that I am actually called to do work. I am supposed to "work out my [own] salvation." *Great*, I think. *Let's get to work. I need to get better at my quiet time. I need to set a schedule for praying throughout the day. I need to be more dedicated to the pursuit of holiness.*

But wait. Paul started this Paul-ishly long sentence with the word "Therefore," which means we should probably take a look at what he is "therefore-ing." Context *always* matters in the Bible. When we go back a few verses, what we find is a doxology in praise of Christ, a glorious description of our great King who humbled Himself to redeem us:

> Have this mind among yourselves, which is yours in Christ Jesus, who, though he was in the form of God, did not count equality with God a thing to be grasped, but emptied himself, by taking the form of a servant, being born in the likeness of men. And being found in human form, he humbled himself by becoming obedient to the point of death, even death on a cross. Therefore God has highly exalted him and bestowed on him the name that is above every name, so that at the name of Jesus every knee should bow, in heaven and on earth and under the earth, and every tongue confess that Jesus Christ is Lord, to the glory of God the Father.
> — Philippians 2:5-11

Do we have *this* King at the forefront of our minds each day while we sweep floors and wipe noses? Do we see ourselves as following in His footsteps and walking in the pattern of humility and service that He first set?

Whose Glory?

The part I tend to forget about is "to the glory of God." Too often, I do the dishes because I like a tidy home and seeing them sitting there is driving me crazy. Because we're having company and nobody wants their home to appear sloppy. Because we honestly don't have any spoons left to use (why is it always the spoons that disappear the fastest??). Then, when I get interrupted from this all-important task of washing the dishes, I simmer in frustration that spills over onto whoever needed me to find something for them or needed their diaper changed.

None of these are entirely bad reasons to wash the dishes, but something important gets revealed about my heart when I become angry at interruptions. One could say that the life of a mother is *made* of interruptions, and it's these interruptions— or rather, our response to them—that shine a light into the crevices of our priorities, our agendas, and ultimately the goal for which we are working so hard.

The Pharisees thought they were doing everything they were supposed to and keeping their homes in good order, so to speak. Yet, as Dane Ortlund points out, "Jesus does not contrast those who clearly reject God's will with those who submit themselves to God's will. Rather, he contrasts those who obey God for the sake of being seen by others with those who obey God for the sake of love for him."[9] Later, he writes, "Mechanized 'obedience' is the problem. Why? Because dutifully resolute obedience so naturally prevents our seeing the need for the cross."[10]

That hits home for me. Sometimes my heart can be farther from God on my good days when I feel like I'm doing everything perfectly than on days when I'm convicted of my own sin and it appears much more clearly outwardly for others to see.

God has designed the utter dependency of small children, the perpetually divided attention, and the variety of unanticipated but pressing claims on our energy (like the toddler desperately needing the shop light to be attached to her trike as a "headlight" right at the moment you had

---

9   Ortlund, p. 49.

10   Ortlund, p. 59.

finally sat down to do some work) to reveal the sins of our hearts.

If I boil over in frustration, or worse, in anger at the person who has dared to interrupt, even if it's for the tenth time that day, something has been uncovered in my heart. When we can organize our days according to our own schedule and all that's really needed is perseverance and discipline to accomplish good results, we can think we pretty much have it together. But we don't.

Anyone who has been a mother *knows* that title comes gift-wrapped along with the very real knowledge that you aren't enough. You don't have all it takes on every early morning, late night, or fiftieth potty-training accident on the trip to the grocery store. Sometimes, you've just had it.

And that's the point. We're born thinking we are enough, that we know better than God, that we can be our own gods. We manifest this in different ways—some of us in subtle arrogance, others in crippling despondency. But we all naturally choose to believe our own narrative, to decide who we are, why we are here, what is important in life. That is why motherhood is a mercy. God, in His utter wisdom and kindness, saw that Eve and every woman after her would need a heart X-ray stuck in front of her face every day of her life to show her that she needed His grace and mercy and unfailing love.

Our responses to the challenges of mothering can show us just the place where the Spirit's work is needed in our hearts, and conversely, the places where He *has* worked in us. Our supernatural patience and perseverance is an evidence of His grace. Right here we see the meeting of Ecclesiastes and the gospel because, at the end of the day, the dishes themselves and whether they're clean or dirty don't matter at all. But those dishes in the hands of God can be instruments used to reveal sin in my life, to sanctify me in the image of Christ, and to bear lasting fruit for eternity in my soul.

Your doing of the dishes to the glory of God, mama, or your long-suffering responses to that which keeps you from doing them, is building toward something of lasting worth.

Filling My Vision

Our justification before the throne of God is established once and for all when our hearts are transformed to place our trust in Christ for salvation before a holy God. Then comes every day after that seminal event, and most of them are not quite so remarkable. But something just as remarkable is being done in the course of our life after salvation and we sometimes miss that part. I think that's why Paul used the weighty phrase "with fear and trembling" to describe how we're supposed to be working out our salvation into the fibers of our hours and days.

The eternal God is transforming us into the likeness of Christ, making us to be the people He intended when He created the first man. He is undoing the effects of the Fall in us and in our homes and our relationships. He is preparing us and this world for heaven, where, with unveiled faces, we will behold His glory and stand before the Father crying, "Holy, holy, holy!" with all the saints and angels.

The very Ecclesiastes-ness of life is meant to show us our own emptiness and press us toward the arms of Jesus who longs to forgive us, to heal us, to fill us. The everlasting God is gentle in heart towards us. Just take a few moments to let that sink in.

The very fabric of motherhood with all its exhaustion and complexity and the way it so completely drains us is actually custom-designed by a wise and loving God to show us our need for His Son. This is true when we are proud and we ignore our need of Him, when we are beaten down and ashamed of our own failures, or just plain forgetful in the midst of trying to remember to change the wash, and not let the baby imperil her life halfway up the stairs, and remind the babysitter that one child inexplicably throws up if she eats pineapple. As that great missionary, Hudson Taylor, wrote:

> *It doesn't matter, really, how great the pressure is… it only matters where the pressure lies. See that it never comes between you and the Lord – then, the greater the pressure, the more it presses you to His breast.*

How would it transform our marriages, our parenting, our relationships with our fellow church members and our neighbors, if we, like Christ, came "not to be served, but to serve"? If we found our joy in obeying the commands of God, in putting to death the deeds of the flesh, in loving and serving those around us, and in "work[ing] the works of [God] while it is still day?" (John 9:4)

The Kindness of Hardship

I've been recently struck by the events surrounding this exhortation by Jesus. Do you remember the healing of the man born blind? The ever-helpful disciples wanted Jesus to tell them whether it was the sin of the parents or of the man himself that had caused his blindness. Jesus straightforwardly told them that it wasn't about this man (or his parents). It was about the glory of God.

Then Jesus spit on the ground, making mud, spread that mud on the man's eyes, and told him to go wash in the Pool of Siloam. The story only gets better as everyone (mostly the Pharisees) try to decide whether the now-seeing man was the same one everyone had seen begging by the side of the road, or whether he had even been blind in the first place.

We come to love this man. He had been a social outcast, a pariah. But when confronted by the Pharisees, those prestigious teachers of the law, he doesn't skip a beat:

> So for the second time they called the man who had been blind and said to him, "Give glory to God. We know that this man is a sinner."
>
> He answered, "Whether he is a sinner I do not know. One thing I do know, that though I was blind, now I see."
>
> They said to him, "What did he do to you? How did he open your eyes?"
>
> He answered them, "I have told you already, and you would not listen. Why do you want to hear it again? Do you also want to become his disciples?"
>
> And they reviled him, saying, "You are his disciple, but we are disciples of Moses. We know that God has spoken to Moses, but as for this man, we do not know where he comes from."
>
> The man answered, "Why, this is an amazing thing! You do not know where he comes from, and yet he opened my eyes. We know that God does not listen to sinners, but if anyone is a worshiper of God and does his will, God listens to him. Never since the world began has it been heard that anyone opened the eyes of a man born blind. If this man were not from God, he could do nothing."
>
> — John 9:24-33

Don't you find yourself cheering for him? He runs circles around the hypocritical, self-righteous, spiritually blind Pharisees. Because of his physical state, he likely hasn't been able to worship in the temple among God's people his entire life.[11] These recorded episodes are the first times he has ever set foot inside the temple. But he's willing to risk it all because of who he thinks Jesus is after only one glimpse of Him. His life has been transformed, and it shows. But the cost to him is very real: "They answered him, 'You were born in utter sin, and would you teach us?' And they cast him out."

Then we see Jesus' love for this man. He heard about the spat with the Pharisees; He heard about the man being cast out, and Jesus went looking for him. He went out on the streets searching and finally found him. Jesus had previously healed his eyes, but now He pursues the heart of a man who had lived his whole life in darkness and been despised by everyone around him.

"Do you believe in the Son of Man?" Jesus asks him.

"And who is he, sir, that I may believe in him?" the man humbly replied.

"You have seen him, and it is he who is speaking to you."

We hold our breath a bit here. Will the man believe Jesus? Will he believe He is actually the Savior for whom everyone has been waiting for hundreds of years—the One who will undo all the brokenness of blind eyes and blind hearts?

"'Lord, I believe,' he said, and he worshiped him."

— John 9:35-38

---

11 Davidson Razafiarivony "Exclusion of the Blind and Lame from the Temple and the Indignation of the Religious Leaders in Matt. 21:12-15," *The American Journal of Biblical Theology* 19 (August 26, 2018): accessed January 17, 2024, https://www.biblicaltheology.com/Research/RazafiarivonyD04.pdf.

This man knew his need and cast all his cares on the One he knew could cause his eyes to truly see, both spiritually and physically. He was given sight by Jesus—real, eternal sight. It was the Pharisees, with their somewhat sarcastic "Are we also blind?" who incurred Jesus' comment, "Your guilt remains."

Using Mud

In general, I feel like my eyes work pretty well. I can tend to believe that my sight is just fine and I plug away at my days forgetting how truly blind I am without the sight the Spirit gives. I forget I need supernatural help to see this world as it truly is.

It's only the kindness of God—grace—that leads us to repentance (Rom. 2:4), and we see this truth every time a bad day brings us to our knees before the throne, begging for forgiveness. We come up against the sin of our own hearts and remember once again that our opinion of ourselves is far too great and our fear of God far too small, and that misplaced loves and desires are yet again leading us astray.

We're spiritually dead and it's only by the enlivening grace of the Spirit of God breathing life into us that we can truly see. That first moment of trust in God, that claiming of Christ as *my* Savior is the first moment of real sight, but that is only the beginning. In that moment, we become eternally right with God, able to please Him rather than anger Him, and the rest of our lives is the working out of that justification into the thoughts and actions and moments of our ordinary lives: in other words, sanctification. We are justified once and for all, but sanctification lasts a lifetime until we meet Jesus in glory and are perfectly renewed in the image of righteousness and holiness (to quote the Westminster Shorter Catechism again).

I think of Jesus spitting on the ground and touching it and making mud. In all honesty, it probably wasn't *nice* mud. There were animals around, people walking places, smelly dust and grime. But that ordinary, unremarkable mud is what a holy God used to heal a man, opening his spiritual eyes to who He really was and redeeming his soul for eternity. Aren't our lives as mothers a lot like this? All the very real dust bunnies under my bed and accumulation of dirty laundry are being used by Jesus to clarify my vision, to help me see Him better, to give me a deeper fear of Him.

The work of motherhood does not redeem us, and we do not somehow magically become better Christians because of the work of keeping a home, just like the man born blind wasn't actually healed by the mud itself. Jesus simply used that mud as a vehicle to accomplish His supernatural work of healing. He is healing us, restoring us every day of our lives and just like with this blind man, He uses ordinary means to do it.

All is vanity—yet God . . . He is doing something in us, through us. In us, the life of Christ is being built using the physicality of the dust and ashes of a fallen world. We are like that blind man and Jesus sometimes literally uses dirt and spit (and other bodily fluids) to remind us of our own need and to open our eyes to His glory and all that He is doing in the world.

The yuckiness of our hearts on the bad Sunday mornings or weekdays is not meant as a punishment. In His hands, these actually become *kindnesses*, used to help us recognize our very real need of forgiveness, of repentance, and of His strength to sustain. As Thomas Watson wrote once, "Better is that sin which humbles me, than that duty which makes me proud." He takes the mud and puts it on our eyes, using something unlovely and useless in itself to open our eyes to His grace. He wants us to run to Him, and He uses unremarkable things to show us Himself. He is tender with us. He is compassionate.

So, weary mama, disillusioned mama, distracted mama, take your gaze to Christ, to the One who died for you and rose for you and lives for you, that you might have abundant, overflowing life. He does not give reluctantly or partly. His arms are wide to welcome you and me; to warm you with His love, and to strengthen you to serve others as He has served you.

5

Who Is Sufficient?

The end of the matter; all has been heard. Fear God and
keep his commandments, for this is the whole duty of
man. For God will bring every deed into judgement, with
every secret thing, whether good or evil.

ECCLESIASTES 12:13-14

Whether we consciously do it or not, our tendency as mothers is often to downplay the value of our work. We sometimes catch glimpses of the beauty and significance in a rare moment of quiet, or when our pastor preaches on the Creation Mandate, or when our children are all blissfully sleeping and we ponder the mystery of eternal souls entrusted to our care.

In the previous chapter, we discussed the significance of the mundane in light of the gospel. But let's look more specifically at the eternal weight of this calling we have as mothers. Our homes really are a mission field, as we raise small humans in the knowledge and admonition of the Lord, and our dedicated work and faithfulness here in this sphere is no less important than preachers of the gospel as we work in each moment of the day to give our children eyes to see God's good news as it really is.

Gospel Triumph

In 2 Corinthians 2–5, Paul contrasts the weaknesses and insufficiency we find so constant in our everyday lives with the realities of what is truly going on as we share the knowledge of Christ with those around us. What other job or calling provides such continual opportunities in such varied scenarios and at every time of day (and night) as motherhood?

Yet we still feel the pull of the world telling us that career milestones, vacation homes, rock climbing proficiency and yearly trips to the tropics are where it's at. We set our face to the plough and what we see in front of us is furrows, and behind us, furrows, and the day is hot and we seem to have done so little at the end of that day, just like the day before that, and the day before that. Our routines are so necessary, yet they sometimes seem to bind us, and we subconsciously feel the transience of it all, even if we can't articulate it fully—or are afraid to, lest we should somehow seem to come out as losers in the grand scheme of things, or even *appear* as losers to those around us.

If you're reading this book during your devotional time, turn to 2 Corinthians so you can read through these chapters for yourself. Or if you just heard the baby wake up, open a Bible app on your phone and play these few chapters while you nurse him. Kids need lunch? Take some time to read even one of these chapters while siblings squabble over a plate of orange slices. They're that good and that rich (Paul's words, not the oranges). On second thought, address the squabbling first and pick up the fallen orange slices, then grab your Bible.

Partway through chapter two of this letter, Paul begins to describe the triumph of the gospel in Christ. God has the final word in all the affairs of men, and He cannot fail to save those who are His. Paul's calling as a minister of the gospel is weighty, as he bears the responsibility to share the hope of Christ with a perishing world. "Who is sufficient for these things?" he asks (2 Cor. 2:16b), and I echo nearly every day. Except he brings up the question out of awe, and I often bring it up out of exhaustion. But can those two things merge? Can exhaustion give way to awe? Keep reading.

Entrusted with a Message

In chapter three, Paul contrasts the temporary old covenant with the perfect new covenant ushered in by Christ's life, death, and resurrection. He speaks specifically of himself and shepherds of God's people as those entrusted with a message, but the truths he writes also apply to every born-again believer. We all, through the power of the Spirit, now bear responsibility as witnesses of this new and perfect covenant which will be fully consummated when Christ returns. "Not that we are sufficient in ourselves to claim anything as coming from us, but our sufficiency is from God, who has made us sufficient to be ministers of a new covenant, not of the letter but of the Spirit." (2 Cor. 3:5-6)

This is not a message we make up or a message about us, but good news entirely outside us. If we try to muster up the strength to bring this message to those around us, we get it wrong. The beauty and glory of the message that Christ has redeemed sinners is so far beyond our frail conceptions of mercy and love and justice that we must continue to learn it each and every day of our lives here on earth until we walk face to face with this wondrous God through eternity.

Paul goes on to explain how this shining, glorious hope doesn't always look like much on this side of eternity. After all, we don't usually walk around feeling like Captain America as we change the poopy diapers of a squirmy infant or read a train book for the hundredth time.

> But we have this treasure in jars of clay, to show that the surpassing power belongs to God and not to us. We are afflicted in every way, but not crushed; perplexed, but not driven to despair; persecuted, but not forsaken; struck down, but not destroyed; always carrying in the body the death of Jesus, so that the life of Jesus may also be manifested in our bodies. For we who live are always being given over to death for Jesus' sake, so that the life of Jesus also may be manifested in our mortal flesh. So death is at work in us, but life in you.
> — 2 Corinthians 4:7-12

We have been entrusted with the souls of future men and women who will live into eternity and we have a handful of years with them to give them a context for these staggering truths. In our homes they can learn frameworks for God's grace and love, or become disillusioned with realities that seem to be empty of truth. In our home they can find the Bible to answer every doubt of their minds and every need of their longing hearts, or they can come to think it trite and overbearing.

> For what we proclaim is not ourselves, but Jesus Christ as Lord, with ourselves as your servants for Jesus' sake. For God, who said, "Let light shine out of darkness," has shone in our hearts to give the light of the knowledge of the glory of God in the face of Jesus Christ.
> — 2 Corinthians 4:5-6

Jesus sets the pattern for all our sacrifices as mothers: the enormous ones and the tiny ones. He who was humiliated from the heights of eternal bliss to death on a cross also grabbed a towel and washed the disciples' mucky feet before dinner. Of all people, Jesus sees what sometimes feels like the humiliation of our lives and He is *with* us in every self-giving, self-draining moment. He not only knows, but He has power to carry us through, to refine and to beautify us through these trials and to bring us into His presence at the end of all time.

What is perhaps more amazing, He also has the power to bring others to Himself through our stumbling obedience. "Since we have the same spirit of faith…" Paul continues,

> We also believe, and so we also speak, knowing that he who raised the Lord Jesus will raise us also with Jesus and bring us with you into his presence. For it is all for your sake, so that as grace extends to more and more people it may increase thanksgiving, to the glory of God.
> — 2 Corinthians 4:13-15

When our children are surrendered in obedience to God rather than clung to and forced into molds of our own making, our moments can bear fruit for eternity. Daily faithfulness is our responsibility. The fruit that comes is up to the Lord. This is where the "rubber" of Ecclesiastes meets the "road" of the gospel. God will indeed "bring every deed into judgement, whether good or evil." We not only serve a God to be feared, but a God who will one day judge all mankind.

Yet this is *our* God, the "One we have waited for," the One who, in Christ, will at the last day declare us righteous, not because of anything at all that we have done or not done, but because Christ Himself was fully obedient to His father on our behalf. "So," Paul finishes,

> we do not lose heart. Though our outer self is wasting away, our inner self is being renewed day by day. For this light momentary affliction is preparing for us an eternal weight of glory beyond all comparison, as we look not to the things that are seen but to the things that are unseen. For the things that are seen are transient, but the things that are unseen are eternal.
> — 2 Corinthians 4:16-18

Treasure in Jars

How then do these truths make their way from the pages of a book to the hearts of our children? The Spirit of God is the only One who can work redemption in their hearts. But as Paul writes in chapter four, God often accomplishes this through the most unlikely of means. Through us. Here are a few contrasts Paul lays out:

As we carry in our bodies the death of Christ	➡	the life of Jesus is manifested in our bodies
As we are being given over to death	➡	the life of Jesus is manifested in our flesh
As our outer self is wasting away	➡	our inner self is being renewed
As we bear light momentary afflictions	➡	an eternal weight of glory is being prepared for us

As our earthly home is destroyed	➡	God is preparing an eternal dwelling for us in the heavens
As we groan, longing to be further clothed	➡	God has prepared us to be swallowed up by life

These contrasts are hard for us to wrap our minds around. We are programmed as fallen humans to love glory, recognition, strength, and ability. But it was in His very weakness and death that Christ's glory was manifest and through His act of humbling Himself to the dust of death that God redeemed a fallen world. Just as Jesus overcame the powers of darkness through taking on mortal flesh, so "the life of Jesus [is] manifested in our mortal flesh." (2 Cor. 4:11) The greatest realities of the universe are shown to be true in our very weakness.

We don't like weakness, need, or insufficiency. Yet we experience these realities every day (and night) and it either begets resentment deep in our bones or drives us "near to the throne of grace, that we may receive mercy and find grace to help in time of need" (Heb. 4:16). If we're not running to the throne, we're drawing from the dry wells of our own adequacy. The sooner we realize that, the sooner joy can germinate in the soil of our days and grow strong vines up the trellis of our time and bear the fruit of the Spirit to be enjoyed by all those around us.

Golden Hour

You see, God did not cause our children to be born into a seminary class where they could learn all the academic answers to every theological question (though those are critically important as well!). He placed them in a home with parents who "groan, being burdened" as Paul puts it in 2 Corinthians 5:4. We long for "what is mortal [to be] swallowed up by life." And the glorious thing? We have a God who "has prepared us for this very thing" and "who has given us the Spirit as a guarantee" (v.5). This is the truth in which we may live out our days if we have the eyes to see. It does not preclude defeating days and battles hard won. We could see it as an afternoon "golden hour" cast over the scenes of war; as the promise of renewal, of coming peace, of joy returning to a fallen world.

This, right here, is the incubator for gospel growth into which God places the image-bearers that are our children. In Christ, God reconciled the world to Himself, then entrusted to *us* the message of reconciliation (2 Cor. 5:19). "Therefore," Paul finishes, "we are ambassadors for Christ, God making his appeal through us . . . Working together with him, then, we appeal to you not to receive the grace of God in vain." (2 Cor. 5:20, 6:1)

As we acknowledge our need of grace and humble ourselves to receive the help God gives, His power is manifested through our lives to those around us, including our children. The truths we speak with our mouths and teach them during Bible time are shown to be really true in their living out. They are given the opportunity to see that "the surpassing power belongs to God, not to us." (4:7) And as we walk through our days relying on the power of the Spirit, they recognize that we live by faith not by sight. Our very weakness as mothers can be that which God uses the most powerfully to draw our children's eyes to the hope that will never disappoint.

Instead of gritting our teeth and "getting through" hard moments and days, what if we saw these moments of vulnerability as opportunities to plant seeds in the hearts of our children which, by God's grace, might bear fruit for eternity? Our goals must be laid down, submitted as sacrifices to God's purposes for our moments and our days. This is not an excuse for laziness but an admission that we are not on our own. That what God is accomplishing in us is not just about us but about what He purposes to do through us.

Clearing Away the Mist

G. K. Chesterton once described the scenario of mist descending on a landscape. It thickens and spreads to every nook and cranny. If a thousand men and horses were to come, they could not begin to collect and carry away all that fog. Yet the sun effortlessly rises and dispels it within the space of minutes. So it is, he wrote, with the work of the Spirit in human hearts. It warms and clears our souls and shows us truth in a way that all our scrambling, striving efforts never could.

There may be other women we look down on, thinking they are well beneath the excellent job we are doing of managing our homes and husbands, or we may look up to other women thinking we could never be as accomplished as they seem to be. But when our gaze is fixed on Christ and on Him above all, we see that He alone radiates all the patience and grace and hope we lack. His mercy and gentleness and steadfast love are what our children, our husbands, our friends, and our fellow church members—what we ourselves—desperately need.

I can bring shovels and buckets (and horses if I happen to have them readily available) into the spiritual and emotional and physical work of each day and slowly, painstakingly, futilely try to clear the mist. Or I can pray that God would warm my cold heart. I can sate my vision with Christ and the soul-filling realities of His gentleness and care toward my weak, sinful heart. I can, as John Piper exhorts, "preach the gospel to myself" day in and day out.

It's only in beholding Him and His loveliness that our hearts can be warmed and strengthened for the tasks of mothering. And it's only in this view that the things of earth both grow strangely dim and are also used by Him to work out salvation in our hearts and (we pray) in the hearts of our children. This "working out" of salvation is hard, but the stakes are eternal.

6

Motherhood as Suffering

Whoever keeps a command will know no evil thing,
and the wise heart will know the proper time and the
just way. For there is a time and a way for everything,
although man's trouble lies heavy on him.

ECCLESIASTES 8:5-6

One hears stories about people who tell the Lord "Send me anywhere but Africa!" and boom! The Lord calls them to be missionaries to a remote tribe in Zambia. I grew up reading dozens of missionary biographies and learning from the missionaries my parents hosted in their home, and the example of their lives and faith deeply shaped me.

From the age of about seven, I was determined that I would *not* spend my life in the States. "Anywhere but here!" I told God in almost as many words. Much of this stemmed from genuine missionary zeal, and some of it from deep hurt experienced in more than one church dissolution. I felt the Lord was choosing to work more powerfully and more visibly overseas than in America, and I wanted to be in the middle of what He was doing. Much of who I was and aspired to become lent itself to the challenges of overseas mission work, and I worked to avoid any rose-colored illusions regarding this calling. But I had learned nothing, it seemed, about the Lord's sense of humor.

Fast-forward ten years and I am *not* living overseas or working as a missionary but, rather, completing seven years of helping equip missionaries, pastors, and publishers through administrative work, mothering full time, and serving as a member of a local church…you guessed it, *in the States.* God was not subservient to my dreams of usefulness, but rather, faithful to reach the unreached parts of my heart that my plan would have exempted.

Not Destination, but Transformation

There is much more to this story, but what has stood out to me over and over as this calling has unfolded is how the Lord chooses for His children their specific fields of work and sanctification. I adapt well to new environments, have reasonable skill in languages, am a motivated person, grew up traveling and experiencing other cultures, received intensive theological training, and am passionate about seeing the gospel spread to the ends of the earth. I was also prepared to be single for the foreseeable future (one memorable conversation with a friend about this mutual resolve came just weeks before both our now-husbands asked us out on our first dates).

On paper, this isn't a terrible résumé for a mission worker, but God isn't primarily looking to hire us for a job to which we might be well suited. Rather, He places us in positions that we know will make us most dependent on His grace and fit us best for eternity.

I know some women who are "natural mothers" and I am not one of them. This isn't to say that motherhood is easy for them or impossible for me, but their personality and their giftedness more naturally run in the nurturing, gentle vein of raising children than mine. There are areas in which I struggle to serve and to give of myself, just as there are other areas in which I find it easier to sacrifice than another person. The calling of motherhood, more than anything else in my life, has thrown me on the grace of God and brought me face to face with my own utter dependence on His strength in a way I truly believe nothing else would have done. It has and is humbling and changing me in deep ways.

I am not claiming that my life is harder than that of a missionary overseas (it's not) or even making a general comparison. I have many friends who are doing both the work of missionaries and motherhood. God formed each of us uniquely and gave us each a unique set of experiences and giftings and He also promises to lend us strength for every calling He gives us. He puts us not in the places we believe we might thrive or accomplish the most, but in the places He desires us to grow and bear fruit for Him. As Charles Spurgeon once wrote, "If any position had been better for you than the one you occupy, divine providence would have put you there."[12] Sometimes, the least visible, most ordinary callings are the ones God uses to accomplish the best work in His people.

Tim Challies, in a striking comment on the man born blind wrote, "He wanted to follow Jesus. He wanted to be close to Jesus. He wanted to live a life of radical obedience. But Jesus told him to stay, not to go. Do not follow me." He continues,

---

12 Charles H. Spurgeon, *Morning and Evening* (Wheaton: Crossway, 2003), November 11.

Christian, God has appointed you to be his missionary right where you are. There is no one better suited to the task. "Go home to your friends, your family, your neighbors, your colleagues, and tell them how much the Lord has done for you, and how he has had mercy on you."[13]

Heaven's Economy

The value of our existence on earth is not measured by what or how much we accomplish, but by what He accomplishes in and through us. "Holiness, not safety, is the goal of our callings," wrote Lilias Trotter in a quotation that hangs on my bedroom wall. Often, we won't know the real value of certain actions or events until eternity.

We're all vessels of clay, and God Himself is the divine Potter. So much of the significance in our existence on this earth lies in who we are becoming, what He is making us into, not what we do or accomplish. The real value of all the years added up lies in a string of actions and moments, some of which might have seemed inconsequential in themselves but which, in His hand, add value to the craftsmanship. Accolades, milestones, accomplishments, which might seem of most significance to the world, may actually matter very little—or even be a "hindrance" to the work He is doing in us.

As Rachel Jankovic writes, "Christ's life given up for others is the centerpiece of our faith. Our life given up for others is the centerpiece of our faithfulness. The glory is that in both cases, death is not the end."[14] What He is building, right now, with our hearts and souls was planned from eternity past and

---

13 Tim Challies, "When Jesus Says Stay," Challies.com (blog), October 24, 2014, https://www.challies.com/christian-living/when-jesus-says-stay/.

14 Rachel Jankovic, *Fit to Burst* (Moscow, ID: Canon Press, 2013), p. 18.

will endure long past the straw and rubble is burned up. The work of His hands in us is His prerogative as the Potter, and His alone. Contrary to what the world might say, there is actually very little value in "self-discovery" or "self-actualization" (though the skills of self-awareness and self-reflection are crucial). God takes care of all that when we are submitted to His will and His way.

That is not to say that our individual personalities and talents and the things that give us a sense of life do not matter. God actually built all these aspects into us when He created us and He knows us in our deepest hearts and souls better than we know ourselves. He can bring a flourishing of gifts we never even knew we possessed and keep us from pursuing opportunities we may think are ideal but will not provide the most fruitful life in the long run. He sees the end from the beginning, and He who fashioned you cares for you in each and every facet of your personhood.

Our very lives, in the minuteness of each day, are lived on the threshold of eternity if we could but glimpse it. We have been redeemed, chosen by the God of the universe, and given a message of hope that every human being in this world, including our children, desperately needs.

The Goal of Hope

We were walking and talking through the neighborhood on a summer day and catching up on life. Donna was an older woman from our church and I was a new mother who had invited her input and mentorship. It had been a hard few weeks, though for no reason that felt justifiable or even definable. The Lord was pressing in on areas of selfishness in my life and it felt like each new moment brought demands to give up, to surrender, to grow in patience. But we were all healthy, life was good, and I felt rather stupid for even admitting I was having a hard time.

Yet Romans 5 had been a tremendous challenge and comfort to me in those days: "Suffering produces endurance and endurance produces character, and character produces hope, and hope does not put us to shame, because God's love has been poured into our hearts through the Holy Spirit who has been given to us" (vv. 3-5).

I brought up these verses and sort of hesitantly said, "I guess it seems like there is an element of suffering in motherhood, though nothing like that endured by persecuted Christians or anything." Donna immediately affirmed what I had shared and said, "No, there is a very real aspect of suffering in being a mother." As we talked further, I started to realize that though the challenges I was experiencing in those days truly weren't comparable to the trials endured by Christians who had been beaten or martyred for their faith, the naming of motherhood as a form of suffering helped me apply the truths of Scripture to what I was facing.

God promises to help those giving up their rights and desires in the cause of obedience. He promises to bear up those who are falling and weak and have no strength—and that is often me as a mother. Our authority as parents brings with it the call to give and give and give to our children just as Jesus has given abundantly and sacrificially to us.[15] It cost Him everything to give us life, and it is fitting that it would also cost

---

15 Jonathan Leeman fleshes out this point excellently in his book *Authority: How Godly Rule Protects the Vulnerable, Strengthens Communities, and Promotes Human Flourishing* (Crossway, 2023), especially pp. 183-95.

us something to bring eternal souls into this world and raise them up into adults.[16]

The calling of motherhood involves a dying to self, a giving up that necessarily causes suffering as sin is killed in our lives and the life of Christ is manifested in us. "Dear Mama," writes Lauren Weir,

> Though you can't seem to get a thing done, something is being done in you…You are a garden of God's tending, and through motherhood, He's cultivating the fruit of your character.
>
> Paul tells us in Romans 5 that character comes on the other side of endurance. Endurance is the secret to that desired fourth soil in the parable of the sower. "As for that in the good soil, they are those who, hearing the word, hold it fast in an honest and good heart, and bear fruit with patience" (Luke 8:15). Hold fast + with patience = endurance…
>
> Rather than taking offense when our sleep or meals or conversations are interrupted we humbly surrender our rights and hold fast: "Let each of you look not only to his own interests, but also to the interests of others. Have this mind among yourselves, that is yours in Christ Jesus" (Phil. 2:4-5).[17]

As mothers, we not only face our own sin, but that of our husbands and our children. We find ourselves amid the general futility of life in a fallen world which groans in the

---

16 Rachel Jankovic winsomely expands on this in her book *Fit to Burst,* pp. 13-18.

17 Lauren Weir (Lauren_Weir), "Dear Young Mama, PT. 1…", Instagram, May 7, 2022, accessed January 18, 2024, https://www.instagram.com/p/CdR9SjMspIp/?hl=en.

pains of childbirth until Christ's return. We see the effects of sin and death within us and all around us and it cannot help but cause us to mourn. Yet these very things are essential tools in the hand of our loving God to wean us off our sin and bring us near to His heart. Lewis once wrote in a letter, "Well, thank God, we shall not be left to the world. All His terrible resources (but it is we who force Him to use them) will be brought against us to detach us from it—insecurity, war, poverty, pain, unpopularity, loneliness. We must be taught that this tent is not our home."[18]

The futility of life in this age isn't just manifest in death itself, but in the daily deaths we experience through interrupted sleep, disrupted schedules, unplanned sickness, and the menial work that fills our days and can feel so beneath us. Jesus gave us His example of living for God's glory in this fallen world. His compassion, humility, faithful obedience, and submission to His Father should all set the pattern for our own days as we seek to see the Fall reversed and the Kingdom come in our hearts and homes.

> Truly, truly, I say to you, unless a grain of wheat falls into the earth and dies, it remains alone; but if it dies, it bears much fruit. Whoever loves his life loses it, and whoever hates his life in this world will keep it for eternal life. If anyone serves me, he must follow me; and where I am, there will my servant be also. If anyone serves me, the Father will honor him.
> — John 12:24-26

---

18 C.S. Lewis, *The Collected Letters of C.S. Lewis, vol. 3, Narnia, Cambridge, and Joy, 1950–1963*, ed. Walter Hooper (San Francisco: HarperCollins, 2009), 1007-8, quoted in *Deeper* (Wheaton: Crossway, 2021), pp. 129-30.

One of the most direct examples of the futility of life in this fallen age is the death of Lazarus. We feel this in Martha's reproachful, heartbroken comment to Jesus, "Lord, if you had been here, my brother would not have died." But Jesus *was* there, and Lazarus' moments in the tomb were numbered.

"I Need Thee"

In light of eternity, our own trials, no matter how big or small, are a blip on the radar. When we cross the threshold of eternity, what has passed before will merely be the prologue, with the rest of the story to come. But on this side, we can get caught up in the "if onlys." If only my baby slept through the night. If only my husband was more attentive. If only I had more time to keep the house clean. If only my child didn't have a life-threatening condition. We can wonder what it is all for, where it's all headed, if there is any purpose in our own or others' sorrows that often seem so unnecessary, almost wasteful.

But if we erase all the trials of our lives, we also erase some of the sweetest lessons the Lord has taught us, the times of deepest closeness to Him, most palpable feelings of His love and care for us (Ps. 94:12-23). Joni Eareckson Tada, who was paralyzed from the neck down at the age of eighteen, writes from the proving ground of this fiery trial:

> No trial, no disease or illness, no accident or injury reaches us apart from God's permission…He has chosen not to heal me, but to hold me. The more intense the pain, the closer His embrace.[19]

---

19   Joni Eareckson Tada et al. "Hidden and Forgotten People: Ministry Among People With Disabilities," Lausanne Committee for World Evangelism, *Lausanne Occasional Paper* no. 35 B, (2004): sec. 4a: https://lausanne.org/docs/2004forum/LOP35B_IG6B.pdf.

In my desire to avoid pain, or to simply be efficient and "make the most" of opportunity, time, or resources, I often railroad right over what God intends as *His* "most" for me or for someone else. As Psalm 33:4 puts it, "For the word of the Lord is upright, and all his work is done in faithfulness."

One of the richest blessings I have received so far as a mother has been a constant sense of my desperation for grace, a real, visceral knowledge of my own insufficiency, the smallness of my own power when left to myself. I cannot forget it: it is right there in front of me every day. The verse "unless the Lord builds the house, they labor in vain who build it," echoes often through the moments of my days. As I climb the stairs, comfort toddler sorrow, and sit down to work after a hectic morning, I find myself breathing snatches of prayers: "Lord, prosper the work of my hands. Lord, grant the increase. Give me wisdom to know how to use my time. Help me faithfully shepherd these hearts in my care."

Charles Bridges put it well when he wrote, "The moment that utter weakness loses its hold, and forgets the need of *habitual* dependence—this is the moment of a certain fall . . . Let thy God, then, [mold] thy will, and he will frame thy happiness. Be thankful that it should be thwarted, even when it pleads most vehemently for indulgence. And shrink not from that process, painful though it be—that [molds] it into conformity with the will of Omnipotent love."[20] Exactly in our moments of weakness are where the Savior of the world loves to meet us and do His most magnificent work.

I recently read that a thirty-seven-year-old stay-at-home mother named Annie Hawks wrote the well-known hymn

---

20   Bridges, pp. 18, 22-23.

"I Need Thee Every Hour," and I can easily believe it. She said later, "I remember well the morning when in the midst of the daily cares of my home, I was so filled with the sense of the nearness of the Master, that wondering how one could live without Him either in joy or pain, these words, 'I Need Thee Every Hour' were ushered into my mind."

I need Thee ev'ry hour,
Most gracious Lord;
No tender voice like Thine
Can peace afford.

I need Thee ev'ry hour,
Stay Thou nearby;
Temptations lose their pow'r
When Thou art nigh.

I need Thee ev'ry hour,
In joy or pain;
Come quickly and abide,
Or life is vain.

I need Thee ev'ry hour,
Teach me Thy will;
And Thy rich promises
In me fulfill.

7

Hope in Childbearing

Cast your bread upon the waters,
for you will find it after many days.

ECCLESIASTES 11:1

In this month of January, we are currently tapping our maple trees for sap to boil down and make maple syrup. Now, before you get all impressed and think we're homesteaders living off the land and only driving into town once a month for small sacks of rice and imported tea, let me rush to explain. This is probably better compared to my childhood entrancement with things I had only read about in books, such as cardinals and fireflies and maple tapping—let loose on the fact that I now live in a place where all these things actually exist.

As it turns out, maple taps can be ordered fairly inexpensively from Amazon, along with blue plastic tubing, and we now have five humble maple taps running from three maple trees into gallon water jugs. We've logged a respectable six gallons of sap in the past couple of weeks (the typical daily flow for one tap for one tree during maple season is about a gallon) and boiled it down to approximately a cup of maple syrup. It looks much more like honey but does taste nice and the small children have approved of it on their morning waffles.

The expertise and labor involved in this process, not to mention the amount of sap needed, has amazed me and also made me want to mop up every last remaining bit of sugary moisture from my plate so it is not wasted. It makes me realize why we pay so much for real maple syrup at the grocery store, and want to talk with some old man who cultivates his own forest of maple trees and gets gallons of sap every year to learn what he knows about this lost art.

Inefficient Faithfulness

The more I think about it, the more this process of maple tapping feels like raising children. In God's wisdom, He has ordained that this endeavor of raising image-bearing humans through every phase of development from embryos all the way to fully-fledged adults making their way in the world is exhausting and draining and demands exponentially more physical, emotional, and spiritual energy than we actually have. A million moments, conversations, responses, and investments go into growing a whole adult who understands how to live in this world, interact with others, and pursue those things which truly matter in life. There is no quick, effortless system, no shortcut, no way of obedience in this pursuit which does not demand that we die to self and pick up our crosses.

Anthony Esolen, in his book *Nostalgia,* writes of children in this way: "The begetting and rearing of children is not instrumental to human goods. It *is* the good for which almost every other one of our activities is, or ought to be, instrumental.["][21] Of course, our primary reason for having children and working as mothers is obedience to God's command at the very beginning of the world. First and foremost, *this* is the means God uses to build His church, to defy the forces of hell—this sometimes unbearably slow, painstaking, laborious work of raising up generations to fear the Lord. There can be no carelessness in this task, no laziness and shortcutting. These are eternal souls in our care and they stand (should the Lord tarry) at the headwaters of generation upon generation which will follow after we are long gone.

Isn't it striking that in this modern age of technology, instant communication, facts at our fingertips, and faster-than-ever ways to heat up lunch, we have nearly forgotten the art of living, of slow things, of the passing on of a lifetime of knowledge and skill? We forget that the Lord of heaven and earth actually stepped into time and defeated death, and that, through us and our families and from the everyday moments of our days, He is extending His reign. As Paul reminded us, this is not merely a physical war, but also a spiritual one. If this task was easier, we might be more tempted to rely on our own strength, to think somehow at the end of the day that we could power through on our own. As it is, we come to face our own insufficiency and need, and this is a deep mercy.

As believers, we defeat time not by following ten principles of entrepreneurs or seven successful tips of housewives to keep a clean home (though these might be helpful at times) but by obeying the Lord of time. The Lord who created time—and us within it—knows how to order His world and we demonstrate

---

21 Anthony Esolen, *Nostalgia*, read by Tom Parks (Brilliance Audio, 2019), Everand, 9hr 47 min.

whether we actually believe that by our obedience or lack of it.

Each of our days begin where the last left off, but also seem somehow like Groundhog Day. Like we're right back where we started and the perseverance of yesterday and the day before and the day before that were all for nothing and the battle lines will remain the same for every new day. As we wake up each day and meet with the King and hear His words and plod through our days seeking to do justly, to love mercy, and to walk humbly with our God, our homes begin to look more and more like outposts of that King, evidences that justice will be done, the wicked will be judged, and the righteous will be vindicated one day.

Wrong will not win out in the end, but every day we must cling to the truth anew. As we become weary in trying to understand everything swirling around us, we must walk into the sanctuary of God to discern the end of it all—the *only* end that makes sense of it all (Psalm 73).

Holding the Line

Our hunger for great patience, greater peace, and more presence of God in our days as we clock into work and roll up our sleeves for another sink full of dishes, send an encouraging text to a struggling friend, and speak gently to a headstrong child—this is where the Kingdom comes. If not here, then nowhere. It is in these little moments that giants of the faith have failed and strayed. Here where we desperately call for grace to be found faithful.

Holding the line is sometimes where the battle is hottest. There are times to advance and move forward, but all that means nothing if the line gives way. We cannot underestimate the need to stay awake in this battle. Every day we need divine grace to remain constant, do the next thing, and continue on the straight and narrow path like Pilgrim in his journey to the Celestial City.[22]

In Deuteronomy, Moses reviewed for the people of Israel the way God had led them out of Egypt and provided for them, how He gave them the Law and spoke to them at Sinai. The glory of God covered the mountain, and the people responded with commensurate reverence.

> This day we have seen God speak with man, and man still live. Now therefore why should we die? For this great fire will consume us. If we hear the voice of the LORD our God any more, we shall die. For who is there of all flesh, that has heard the voice of the living God speaking out of the midst of fire as we have, and has still lived? Go near and hear all that the LORD our God will say, and speak to us all that the LORD our God will speak to you, and we will hear and do it.
> —Deuteronomy 5:24-27

We have moments like this, where we realize the splendor of our God and it makes us want to worship Him, to believe Him, and to do whatever He says. Nobody stands on the edge of the Grand Canyon and thinks, *boy, this is kinda lame.* The truth is, I think that often while I'm wiping up chunks of squash and other things which I will not mention off the floor under the baby's high chair. Both of these things, the Grand Canyon and motherhood, are works of the Lord, and yet one

---

22 From John Bunyan's, *Pilgrim's Progress,* known and loved by generations of Christians.

of them brings out our awe and wonder and the other often brings out grumbling.

Turns out, the Israelites' fear of the Lord didn't last long either. Just a little while later, they were complaining about how long Moses was taking on the mountain and donating all their jewelry for the making of an idol. Peter Craigie, commenting on this quick change of events writes, "The reverence shown now was in response to the phenomena accompanying God's revelation, and though it was not thereby any less genuine, it was nevertheless regrettable that the people could not show the same reverence in the more mundane affairs of daily life."

Do we show right reverence for God in the everyday affairs of our lives as mothers? Are there areas of your life where it is easy to honor the Lord and areas where you grumble and complain and allow idols of self or comfort or goals to take the place of God? We often have our own ideas of what obedience *should* look like, while ignoring the areas of obedience to which we are actually called.

Elisabeth Elliot puts it best when she writes,

This job has been given to me to do.
   Therefore, it is a gift.
   Therefore, it is a privilege.
   Therefore, it is an offering I may make to God.
   Therefore, it is to be done gladly, if it is to be done for Him.
   Here, not somewhere else, I may learn God's way.
   In this job, not in some other, God looks for faithfulness.

Redeeming Earthliness

Before sin ever entered the world, God gave us the dominion mandate: Be fruitful and multiply and fill the earth. God designed us among all His creatures to display His glory and to spread His fame over the whole earth. This multiplication of mankind was twisted as man forsook the Creator and sought to make his own way to heaven. Yet woven into the very curse was the germ of new life, the promise of a child who would come and redeem all things and heal all sorrow.

Millennia later, Jesus came to earth as the Son of God and Man, clothed in the same flesh and blood as the man and woman who first received the dominion mandate. He ransomed a people for Himself "born not of blood nor of the will of the flesh nor the will of man, but of God". Right here is where the almost cynical references in Ecclesiastes run into the tide of gospel hope not yet fully realized by the writer.

We live in tension. Maybe you've felt this, even subconsciously, as you step out of a sermon your heart needed in order to deal with a child's fit or have an argument with your spouse just after a particularly rich quiet time. Our very lives are a dichotomy, bearing in them the stamp of the old Adam who fell and instilled us with sin in the core of our being, and the new Adam who redeemed us and will preserve us until we behold Him in sinless glory.

In His redeemed descendants, Christ now extends His dominion throughout all the earth, commissioning them to "Go therefore and make disciples of all nations, baptizing them in the name of the Father and of the Son and of the Holy Spirit, teaching them to observe all that I have commanded you (Matt. 28:19-20a)." By the Fall, we were removed from the life-giving, vital force of God's presence. Now, the Spirit of God has come to dwell among we who believe, enlivening our dead hearts, empowering us both to live in obedience as His disciples and to make new disciples. Enabling us to be mothers.

"And behold, I am with you always, to the end of the age" (Matt: 28:20b), he says to us, as we wake up early to crying babies and work on computers with small people crawling over our shoulders and endeavor to be patient as our morning time in the Word is cut in tenths. Before the Fall ensured pain in childbearing and the chafing of selfish desires and the fragility of our identity, God gave us, as women, the responsibility to bear and to raise children, and to aid our husbands in the dominion mandate.

In this very work of bearing children and nurturing life and welcoming others into our homes and lives for gospel work, we stand with Christ and against the forces of darkness. At its core, this calling is *good*; it is worthy of all our highest skill and aspiration. Here in the home begins the incubation of the glory of God as it unfolds itself in the hearts of small image-bearers and in our own lives as we are sanctified back into divine resemblance.

That Which Is Unseen

This hearkening back to Eden in our calling as mothers gives us both realism and hope. We are actually laboring under a curse, and we feel this in a multitude of ways each day. Everything under the sun is vanity and will one day pass away. Yet there is also an inherent *goodness* in our work—the building of something real and lasting and eternal in us and in our families and neighbors and churches that will one day be revealed for what it truly is. As we read in 2 Corinthians 3:18a, "And we all, with unveiled face, beholding the glory of the Lord, are being transformed into the same image from one degree of glory to another."

Our "Ecclesiastes" work of motherhood is as mundane as painting rooms and as glorious as winning souls. As women, we have been specially designed by God to be life-bearing and life-sustaining and to mirror Him in this particular way more than men. We hold in our arms and in our homes and in our very bodies that tantalizing, agonizing divide between heaven and earth, between that which is seen and that which is unseen but will one day fill all reality.

The writer of Ecclesiastes poetically writes, "Cast your bread upon the waters, for you will find it after many days" (Eccl. 11:1). About this verse, Bridges comments, "The many days between seed-time and harvest are days of special anxiety—hoping seeming impossibilities—believing paradoxes. But the promise is God's own living truth; and it will be found not the less sure for the delay. And when waiting days have done their work, humbling us in entire dependence upon God, and ripening us for the harvest of blessing in due season…We shall reap, if we faint not."[23]

I am reminded of the Old Testament people of God who continually lived among the shadows of what was to come. The entire sacrificial system prefigured Christ, but they didn't yet know how God would redeem His people—them—and lived in the straining morning light of a sun that had not yet risen. The prophets of the Old Testament continually called out to Israel to remember their God and His power and faithfulness, despite their limited knowledge of His planned redemption and the undeniable power of the forces that faced them. In his book, *A Time for Confidence,* Stephen Nichols writes, "Where the people mistook the shadows for the eternal and abiding

---

23   Bridges, p. 266.

reality, the prophets saw beyond the shadows and saw straight into the truly real."[24]

We have lessons to learn from these men and women who persevered in faith. Instead of sacrificing baby goats, we now have Christ and the tangible hope of the gospel. We await Christ's return to make all things right. Later in his book, Nichols writes, "We must consider Jesus because our challenges are so great. We can stand firm because Jesus is so much greater."[25]

The labors of our hands, while they may seem vain and pointless in the moment are, surrendered to the Lord and by the power of the Spirit, building an eternal weight of glory that we will one day see for what it truly is.

---

24   Stephen J. Nichols, *A Time for Confidence* (Orlando, Reformation Trust, 2016), p. 3.

25   Ibid., p. 74.

The Apologetic
of Motherhood

*Better is a handful of quietness than
two hands full of toil and a striving after wind.*

ECCLESIASTES 4:6

It's a Saturday morning in January and I sit writing by the window, watching cars go by and enjoying the warmth of a fire. My husband, Caleb, is making waffles with my oldest, and the younger troublemaker is napping. That's the Instagram version. Want to hear the real version?

The baby was up, as usual, around five o'clock and wouldn't go back to sleep with coaxing from a pacifier or a bottle. So into bed with me she came and settled down instantly. Impishly. For a while, things were blissful. I crept down to the kitchen and made a cup of tea, bringing it back up with my Bible and a devotional book. A few pages in, the baby woke up and crawled around grabbing things, giggling, and not being sleepy at all. So much for my Bible time.

We played quietly, then went downstairs, where I changed her diaper and started to clean the kitchen. If you've ever had one, you know that babies like to help clean the kitchen by standing at your feet, grabbing dirty dishes out of the dishwasher, and climbing on the open door. If they decide this is uninteresting, they move on to anything they know they are not supposed to do. It had been about an hour and a half since the baby woke up and interrupted *my* restful Saturday morning, and I thought it was about time my husband was done with *his* rest also, so I yelled out, "I could use some reinforcements down here, babe!"

He finally emerged and, a few minutes later, the toddler did as well. Meanwhile, I was tidying up the incessant mess, trying to load the dishwasher and becoming increasingly annoyed at the baby for being a baby. I knew my heart was in the wrong place. I knew the problem was not the mess or the house or my tired husband (for the record, he always makes sure I get more sleep than he does, which makes the whole thing more awful). The problem was my heart and I knew it.

Preaching the Gospel to Ourselves

Ironically, the day before I'd been reading a book on marriage which addressed the pattern of sin taking over our hearts, as it did in me this morning. Dave Harvey, in *When Sinners Say "I Do"*, writes, "Your warring, sinful desires come out swinging. Why? Because their purpose is to keep you from doing the things you want to do for God."[26] If my husband had woken up before me and made me tea, if the baby had slept in until eight, if the house had been cleaned professionally the day before,

---

26 Dave Harvey, *When Sinners Say "I Do"* (Wapwallopen: Shepherd Press, 2007), p. 49.

then I probably would have been perfectly happy. Or maybe not. I'm sure there are women in the world (maybe even you) who think, *If only I was married, I could be happier; if only I had children; if only my husband wasn't working on Saturday mornings; if only I had a dishwasher.*

"Man's nature…," reflected John Calvin, "is a perpetual factory of idols." We will *always* find something with which to manufacture idols and give them the allegiance of our time and energy and love instead of the God who redeemed us. In a passage speaking of marriage, which can easily be applied more broadly, Harvey puts it like this, "The cause of our marriage battles, friends, is neither our marriage nor our spouse. It's the sin in our hearts—entirely, exclusively, without exception."[27]

All events of this particular morning were opportunities for my heart to demonstrate that I had been redeemed; that because Christ had sacrificed Himself for me, I could sacrifice myself for others. I did not have to seek recognition or ease or my own agenda. I could lay down my rights because He laid down His and showed me how. He came from the heights of glory. And I? Well, I was only awakened from my sleep an hour or two early on a Saturday morning. Who do I think I am, anyway?

Do I think I am above changing diapers? Above getting up earliest, changing that last load of laundry (the one you forget about until you've already fallen into bed dog-tired at eleven-thirty)? Jesus wasn't above the most menial tasks, yet somehow His example of humility rolls right off my back and fails to sink into my bones. I feel I'm owed more, that my skills should be more valuable than to be used on endless dishes and grimy bathrooms.

---

27 Ibid., p. 51.

More Significant

Some days are wonderful and the sense of purpose is palpable. We are, in the words of Paul, "set apart as holy, useful to the master of the house, ready for every good work."

All too often, that reality is forgotten and my grumbling, resentful heart rears its ugly head. *I remember the days I could leave the house for the day with a grand total of three items. Now it's five hundred and three. Why am I the person who has to pack everything for our family vacation and my husband can't remember the two things I asked him to grab?* On and on.

Truly insignificant things suddenly loom large and I am faced with a choice: do I humble myself, allow myself to be expended in menial ways, to be endlessly needed and demanded and "used" by those God has entrusted to my care? Do I do this joyfully, seeing this expenditure of my time and energy and very life as the glorious and noble calling it is? Or do I see it, in that particular moment, as a life I never wanted?

Christ calls us to count others as more significant than ourselves, to lay down our lives and take up our crosses. Did we think this was going to be pleasant? Did we think it was like a hard paper at college: hard, but totally doable given enough coffee and an all-nighter or two? I'm guessing you, like me, may have underestimated the messiness and hardship of actually letting go of self-interest, truly seeking the good of others more than my own, and having many inconvenient opportunities to demonstrate these professions.

This road of cross-bearing looks different for each person, but as Jesus walks beside us on this road of sanctification, He loves us too much to let us walk the pleasant way to glory. See, the funny thing is, I never thought I was a selfish or angry person while I was living on my own. In fact, I had some of the richest personal devotion times with my own, unswiped-at-by-toddlers cup of *hot* coffee in the morning after a full night of sleep. They were *fantastic*, let me tell you. Then, after being married and having a few children, I somehow became more selfish and more prone to anger, if only in my heart.

You know that's not how it is. Rather than *making* me a selfish person, contact with other sinners simply brought what was already there. I had these diseases in my heart from day one, but marriage and motherhood are God's mirrors to help me see the realities of my sin-sick heart that I had ignored or never even knew existed.

Christ's blood seals us for the day of redemption and our election is sure. Nothing can take us from the Father's hand. But justification is only the beginning of our journey of sanctification as God slowly restores in us the image of Christ which was so marred by the Fall. In a strange, unfathomable way, we are simply becoming who we already are, coming to live consistently with our real identity as God's children. This morning was simply the next lesson in that school—and I failed the test.

Does that seem like a strange way to put it? We don't like to think of God as "testing" us. It sits strangely. After all, God loves us unconditionally, right? And He knows all things, so why would He need to test us to know what is in our hearts? These revealing tests are primarily a mercy to us, opening a window on our hearts, reminding us of both our need and His offer of "grace to help and mercy in time of need."[28]

28   Craig Riggall, "Put to the Test," December 11, 2022, Camp Hill, PA, 43:32, https://www.sermonaudio.com/solo/grbcws/sermons/1217222212434995/.

Already Done

Christianity is not a religion about learning how to pass divine tests. It is a religion that shares the good news that all the tests have already been passed. Our obedience, just like our disobedience, can contribute nothing to our standing before God.

As Michael Reeves wrote in his book *God Shines Forth*,

> If we are not captured specifically by the glory of God in Christ and propelled outward in happy proclamation of the one who has freely given himself to us, then it will be no surprise when our message quickly has little to do with him. If it is not *him* we are enjoying, it will not be *him* we convey to others. Even unwittingly, we may become ministers of another gospel (Gal. 1:7).[29]

Christianity does not call us to asceticism or moralism or indulgence or more intentional "mindfulness."[30] It calls us, first and foremost, to bring our failure—nothing else, and trade it in for Christ's perfect righteousness.

This is the gospel of hope. The only thing that is truly good news amid the failures, the pain, the disappointments, and even the mundanity of our lives. This is the gospel we must preach day in and day out to ourselves and to our children in every moment of every day. This Christ is the only One who

---

29   Michael Reeves, *God Shines Forth* (Wheaton: Crossway, 2022), Everand.

30   Defined by the Mayo Clinic as "a type of meditation in which you focus on being intensely aware of what you're sensing and feeling in the moment, without interpretation or judgment." "Mindfulness exercises," *Mayo Clinic* online, October 11, 2022, https://www.mayoclinic.org/healthy-lifestyle/consumer-health/in-depth/mindfulness-exercises/art-20046356#:~:text=Mindfulness%20is%20a%20type%20of,mind%20and%20help%20reduce%20stress.

can bring meaning and fill us with joy. Apart from Him, we can do nothing.

Praying for Jealousy

During the first spring and summer after moving to our home in Pennsylvania, we discovered dozens of new flowers and bushes blooming around the property. Along with the flowers, we inherited an elderly neighbor who liked to come and sit on a bench in our backyard during his regular walks. Sometimes, he'd bring a book with him; sometimes, he'd just sit and look out at the garden and the birds and enjoy the sunshine.

His name was George, and he was a character if you ever met one. In his prime, he had been sharp as a tack, no doubt about it. This natural intelligence was interspersed with moments of, well, I was never sure exactly what. He was a man of big ideas and expansive vision. If what he said was accurate, he had helped invent computers, had done business with some of the foremost minds of his day, had started a business which rented space in the Twin Towers just days before 9/11, and had opened with his saxophone for the likes of Frank Sinatra.

He still read and watched a great deal, it seemed, and was often eager to introduce anyone who would listen to his latest idea: a global cooperative that would save every family hundreds of dollars a month and would be backed by a bond that he invented. He had just called up "Diane" on the board of the UN that afternoon to discuss the idea.

George lived in a rundown old house one street over, along with a few other people. He had never married, and when asked if he ever regretted that, said he had seen some happy families and some miserable families and didn't regret avoiding the possibility of the latter. "The girls had been kind to him" in his day, and he seemed content with that. As our conversations developed, it turned out he had been raised Catholic but had long since abandoned any belief in God. He was a man of science and, he argued, there was simply not enough evidence for an all-supreme Deity.

I pressed a bit, pointing out that this was a big risk to take with eternity in the balance. What if he was wrong? What then? No one could possibly know all the facts, discover all the science, or draw perfect conclusions. In the end, we all place our trust in something. Was he ready to eternally trust his own conclusions about God and the Bible, even though he'd never even read it?

He often re-directed the conversation, sidestepped questions, and became downright rude in one particularly forthright interaction. It became clear that he simply couldn't face the possibility of having been mistaken about life, about the joys of family, about the existence of God Himself. He hid behind his intellect, but even that was waning. I could sense glimmers of a slightly intimidating man, but mostly he was just pitiable.

A stay-at-home mom can often feel isolated from normal evangelistic opportunities, even while realizing her children are her primary mission field. I had to smile at God's providence in literally sending an opportunity for evangelism onto my back patio. As I got to know him, my prayer for George became that he would see something attractive in our normal, backyard lives. I prayed that our interactions would stay with him and that, even if he blew me off in conversation, he wouldn't be able to shake some of the questions I asked. I wanted him to see something in our lives that he had never tasted and become unbearably jealous. I wanted our family to be an aroma of Christ to one who was, most certainly apart from the intervening grace of God, perishing.

Apologetic to a Hopeless World

Though it is sometimes hard to remember on days when everyone seems out of sorts and things are just "off," or days when we're deeply struggling to believe the promises of God, our every moment is pervaded by an eternal hope every unbeliever lacks on their best days. We have unshakeable hope, solid truth, and a certain future which cannot be taken from us. I find it takes reminding myself of these realities, actively meditating on the Word, and setting Christ before my distractible gaze to keep these things at the forefront of my mind. As mothers, we can get so caught up in the endless list of things waiting on us to do them, to wipe them, to hug them, that we forget the bigness of our God.

What if we lifted our gaze to see the opportunities right in front of us, the chances for ministry to the grocery store clerk, the receptionist at the doctor's office? The more we steep our souls in the glorious gospel of Christ, the more it will overflow to those around us in a patient interaction with a determined child, a smile to the person on the sidewalk, or taking the time to ask how the grocery clerk's day is going. We might be surprised at what we find.

When John D. Rockefeller, estimated to have been the richest individual in US history, was asked, "How much money is enough?" He replied, "Just a little bit more."[31]

Similarly, in a moment of remarkable honesty, Tom Brady admitted, "Why do I have three Super Bowl rings and still think there's something greater out there for me? … I think, '… it's got to be more than this.' I mean this isn't, this can't be what it's all cracked up to be…"[32]

More than we'd guess, the world senses there is more to life than they see. They feel there *has* to be! There are dozens of ways they pursue this hope, but you, mother, as you live out your gospel hope in the midst of your mundane life can point them to an eternal hope. Christ fills us every day with the same hope so desperately needed by every unbeliever we meet in the course of our days.

A pastor of mine once said that the difference between us and the animals is that they are pushed by their past, while we are pulled by our future. Some doubt there even is a future. Death can feel far removed from our sequenced lives, and this is not necessarily always a benefit. Sometimes, the presence of death gives those living a keener sense of the meaningless wind that runs through the heart of this world apart from its Maker.

---

31 Tom Nicholas and Vasiliki Fouka, "John D. Rockefeller: The Richest Man in the World," Harvard Business School, Case 815-088 (Abstract), December 2014 (Revised March 2018), https://www.hbs.edu/faculty/Pages/item. aspx?num=47167#:~:text=Rockefeller%20(1839%2D1937)%2C,American%20 business%20and%20economic%20history.

32 Tom Brady, "Tom Brady, Part 3," interview by Steve Kroft, CBS News, November 4, 2005.

Setting Our Hearts

Even as Christians, we can taste and swallow the lies of the world and think them a little sweet. We can wonder if happiness is not found in a line of work, or the perfect companion, or a more freeing lifestyle, or anything else we happen to glimpse on Instagram—forgetting that a full feed can sometimes cover over an empty soul. It can be said that most often, that which is best for the soul is not apparent to the eyes:

> For all that is in the world—the desires of the flesh and the desires of the eyes and pride of life—is not from the Father but is from the world. And the world is passing away along with its desires, but whoever does the will of God abides forever.
> — 1 John 2:16-17

> As many were astonished at you—his appearance was so marred, beyond human semblance, and his form beyond that of the children of mankind—so shall he sprinkle many nations. Kings shall shut their mouths because of him, for that which has not been told them they see, and that which they have not heard they understand.
> — Isaiah 52:14-15

Might we be wiser, as the people of God, to click less for the pleasure of our eyes and set our hearts on the eternal things that the Spirit of God supernaturally enables us to crave? Are we pulled throughout our days by the reality of a returning King? As Reeves writes, "Our mission carries the same glory as our hope."[33]

---

33 Reeves, Everand.

Amid even the happiest of times, we touch the shallow bottom of worldly joys and sense the charade. Gods of our own making taunt the frustration of our hearts and the Word lies untrusted. The pursuit of fulfillment and the empty ache is endless. We are restless creatures until we find our rest in the One through whom, by whom, and for whom we were all created. Only there will we find an anchor for our existence, for the existence of the person next to us in line at Starbucks, and even for the worth of the unborn.

Having found Him who is the rest of our souls, may we as Christians step out into the wind of discomfort and emptiness to meet those whose hearts ache even in seeming success and happiness. It may be that those who sorrow are closest to the answer and those most confident in their own answers are the most in need of assurance that this world is passing away.

Along with all its beautiful desires.

But there was One sent to this earth two thousand years ago as a servant to carry the sins of His own people and, as their King, to subdue us to Himself, rule and defend us, and conquer all His and our enemies (paraphrased from the Westminster Shorter Catechism, answer 26). This Christ—have you heard? In Him all that is best and most joyful becomes a reality once again. In Him, the vanity of our existence melts away like mist, revealing the glory of eternity which He is preparing for us and for which He is preparing us:

> Give attention to me, my people,
>   and give ear to me, my nation;
> for a law will go out from me,
>   and I will set my justice for a light to the peoples.
> My righteousness draws near,

my salvation has gone out,

and my arms will judge the peoples;

the coastlands hope for me,

and for my arm they wait.

Lift up your eyes to the heavens,

and look at the earth beneath;

for the heavens vanish like smoke,

the earth will wear out like a garment,

and they who dwell in it will die in like manner;

but my salvation will be forever,

and my righteousness will never be dismayed.

—Isaiah 51:4-6 (emphasis mine).

9

The Magic of Simple

*Behold, what I have seen to be good and fitting is to eat and
drink and find enjoyment in all the toil with which one toils
under the sun the few days of his life that God has given him,
for this is his lot. Everyone also to whom God has given wealth
and possessions and power to enjoy them, and to accept his lot
and rejoice in his toil—this is the gift of God. For he will not
much remember the days of his life because God keeps him
occupied with joy in his heart.*

ECCLESIASTES 5:18-20

*And I commend joy, for man has nothing better under
the sun but to eat and drink and be joyful, for this will go
with him in his toil through the days of his life that God
has given him under the sun.*

ECCLESIASTES 8:15

I have remembered a sentence about biscuits from a book
I read nearly three years ago. Surprisingly, it wasn't a cookbook,
but a book on motherhood. The author, Rachel Jankovic, was

illustrating the joy that should overflow from our faith in Christ to those around us in tangible ways. Like the servants given talents in Matthew 25, we have been given salvation as a treasure to *use* and to multiply.

She writes, "Our Master did not give us this gold of forgiveness so that we might hide it. He wants us to use it. He wants us to make things happen with it. He wants us to take our salvation and turn it into biscuits hot on the table. He wants us to take our salvation and turn it into contagious joy; into sacrifice for others."[34]

Our sacrificial service shouldn't be grudging or tinged with selfishness, but open-handed, extravagant. We should take delight in laying down our lives for our families even in ways that aren't absolutely necessary because of the abundance of our love for them. Rather than obligated drudgery, those flaky biscuits signaled the overflow of Rachel's heart's delight in redemption from sin as she served those God had given into her care.

A Season of Biscuits

This isn't an excuse to look *only* for the spreading-butter-on-a-hot-biscuit ways to care for others, since genuine service is often far less pleasant. However, it does mean that, as homemakers, we are tasked with seeking out ways to create an environment of settled, grounded belonging and joy, which will anchor the hearts and lives of our husbands and children. This is a sacred and beautiful calling but one that is often either ignored or idolized.

---

34 Jankovic, p. 22.

In fact, the translation of our husband's paycheck into food on the table, clothes on bodies and a comfortable home is our privilege and responsibility as wives, mothers, and homemakers. We put his love, vision, care, and provision into concrete terms for them[35], mirroring how we receive the gifts of the Father through the work of the Spirit. The work of our husbands as they provide, protect, lead, and shepherd our homes can often be forgotten as we labor through our own lessons and to-do lists. A godly husband provides the safety, framework, and freedom for our own realms of duty.

To state the obvious, the point of our homemaking is the people for whom we are making the home. As Charles Bridges puts it, "Splendid services are not always required; but acts of kindness to the weakest and meanest of his people, worked out in the true spirit of love to himself."[36] We can err on the side of Martha Stewart and make sure that each throw pillow is in place and each rug free from dog hair before making blanket forts and inviting someone new over (thereby ensuring that we never do). Or we can err on the side of the gnostics, claiming that insignificant things like painting a room or making dessert at midnight with our husband aren't worth the trouble and we're made for more ethereal things.

There's a grain of truth in both these extremes. As humans, we were made fit for realities that far surpass what our senses take in. Yet God put Adam in a garden, of all earthly things, and told him to guard and keep it. I imagine Adam and Eve's days were split between the ethereal experience of walking with God Himself and standing barefoot in the cool, dark

---

35 I am indebted to Rachel Jankovic for this profound point (Jankovic, p. 57).
36 Bridges, p. 269.

earth of Eden to prune vines, harvest food, and clear paths. What does this mean for us? Obviously, a mother of several small children cannot spend every evening obsessing over a beautiful table setting, but have you ever tasted the bliss of that bowl of ice cream on the couch after the children are both in bed *and* asleep?

A neighbor of mine has started a "Supper Club" where she hosts themed, many-course dinners for special events as a side business. They are elaborate affairs with careful thought put into the lighting, floral arrangements, and live music. I imagine the wedding supper of the Lamb, which we all await, will have echoes of dinner parties just like the ones she hosts, but with all the satisfaction of that hard-earned bowl of store-bought ice cream.

Tending Our Gardens

As we keep our homes, we inherit the calling of the first man and woman to tend a garden, and we, no less than they, answer to the God who gave us that sphere of service. The fear of the Lord keeps us from becoming either overwhelmed or lazy. Order, cleanliness, and beauty all flow from God, and we are given inspiration and motivation in these things as we reorient our gaze continually back to Christ who is the reason for everything. We imitate the Maker of the garden when we wash a car seat cover, plant a new garden, and teach a child to cut with a knife.

These tasks considered on their own are not the ultimate calling of our lives, but they make up the realm of that calling and give it shape and form. As Rachel Woodham put it in a helpful article, "With a sacramental vision, the kitchen is no longer the thing that takes me away from important work. It is the work. It is Reality."[37] In this, we are freed from our own small vision of duty into broader, wider opportunities.

No matter the season in which we find ourselves, we can make it our mission to capture small pieces of the festivity of heaven throughout our days: big bowls of buttery popcorn on a day when the rain just won't stop—literally or figuratively. Trying an outlandish recipe because our husband said he thought it looked good. Driving the pickup truck into the woods on a fall day with the newest haul of library books, blankets, and a thermos of hot cocoa. Looking into the eyes of a trying child and smiling fully at them, then finding something to make them laugh. Gazing up into the sky on a clear winter night. There are a million simple, inexpensive, ordinary ways curated by your own experience, skill set, personality, and geography to cultivate wonder, delight, and contentment in the life God has given you.

There is a balance to both the delights and the responsibilities of our lives and it is the way of wisdom to find this balance. Either one in excess becomes grotesque: the unkempt home of one who runs after whatever is entertaining and fun in the moment; or the stringent home of one obsessed with a pristine environment above all else. Restraint and abandon are both necessary in their own time and place, for we serve a God who loves both extravagance and order. Rhythms and routines are built into the creation order but also the wasteful extravagance of leaves in autumn, excessive displays of stars, and exuberant streaks of bioluminescence in the ocean.

---

37   Rachel Woodham, "How Then Shall We Cook?," Circe Institute (blog), August 2, 2023, https://circeinstitute.org/blog/how-then-shall-we-cook/.

Are we like the farmer who is slow to plant his seeds and lazy at the proper time to harvest (Prov. 10:4)? Or are we always so busy planting and harvesting that we never quite find time to "eat, drink and be merry" (Eccl.3:22)? Understanding our own tendencies can help us place areas of needed growth before the Lord. Overindulgence of either work or rest can quickly become distortions of our callings. Even before the Fall, we were given work as something innately good, but we were also inherently limited as humans. This means we can accept both our calling and our capacity as given by the Lord and as opportunities for humility and dependence on Him.

Here again, the truth of Ecclesiastes speaks into our callings. For everything there is a season, a right place and time. It is the way of wisdom to discern those seasons. I often pray a simple prayer at the beginning of the day that God would help me understand the best way to spend my time, and that my priorities would be in line with what He most wants me to accomplish in a day. Sometimes that is paperwork, sometimes cooking a particularly nice dinner, sometimes cooking no dinner at all and striving to show patience to a headstrong child who *will* have her own way and must be taught that the way of blessing is actually in obedience. To paraphrase Ecclesiastes, there is a time to diaper, and a time (blessedly), to rest from diapering.

Singer and songwriter Caroline Cobb put it like this:

In God's Kingdom, success is about being faithful with what we have. Our job is to take the little pile of seeds God has given us and plant them in the little plot of land that God has put in front of us to cultivate. Then we trust Him to let them take root and bear harvest—sometimes a harvest we never get to see.[38]

Glimpses of Satisfaction

I recently read the autobiography[39] of a renowned chef who began her account with the magical memories of magnificent outdoor summer feasts her parents threw for friends and neighbors. Drinks were laid to chill in the nearby creek, meat roasted on a sizzling spit, and her mama in the kitchen sang while she cooked in an elegant dress and heels. The specific tastes, smells, and feelings of those magical evenings threaded like a siren call throughout the rest of her catastrophic adolescence and successful adulthood. It was as if every day afterwards was a searching to regain the perfect feeling of those moments as a child.

Isn't that like all of us? We catch glimpses of what we were made for throughout our lives and we spend the rest of our days trying to attain it. C.S. Lewis captures this intangible feeling best in his brilliant book, *Till We Have Faces*:

The sweetest thing in all my life has been the longing — to reach the Mountain, to find the place where all the beauty came from... — my country, the place where I ought to have been born. Do you think it all meant nothing, all the longing? The longing for home? For indeed it now feels not like going, but like going back.[40]

---

38 Quoted in Tim Keesee, *A Day's Journey* (Minneapolis, Bethany House Publishers, 2023), p. 148.

39 Gabrielle Hamilton, *Blood, Bones, and Butter* (London, Chatto Chatto & Windus, 2011).

40 C.S. Lewis, *Till We Have Faces* (Orlando, Harcourt, Inc., 1956), pp. 75-76.

Snatches of this joy flash through in late nights of laughter and drinks and conversation with good friends when someone all of a sudden realizes it's ten o'clock but nobody wants to go home. In watching our sleeping babies with their diapered bottoms in the air and their chubby faces pictures of smooshy tranquility that threaten to make our hearts burst. In sun-warmed bowls of fuzzy summer peaches on the kitchen counter perfuming the air with their sweet fragrance.

Undeniably, direct effects of the Fall are all around us in death, disease, heartache. These are not to be rejoiced in, but mourned over as wrongs that will one day be righted when King Jesus returns. But do we include too much of life in this fallenness? Do we fail to recognize the inherent goodness of work as God sees it? Do we devalue the unglamorous and perhaps distasteful tasks of each day and lose their momentous, eternal significance?

Meaningful Repetition

Our culture is full of immediacy, instant gratification, and short-sided vision in a staggering loss of the majestic sweep of history and rich tradition. Modern moments close in on us rather than fitting us to live in our present season as the thread of our most ordinary days is woven into a tapestry of beauty and richness. From the beginning of the world, God has used everyday labors and repetition as a tool for the building of His kingdom, yet we forget this in the cheapness and immediacy of the present age. "While the earth remains, seedtime and harvest, cold and heat, summer and winter, day and night, shall not cease" (Gen. 8:22).

Grand things are made by the accumulation of small moments, rapt attention. Entire reefs built by tiny polyps can be seen all the way from the moon. Cathedrals in Europe were built by multiple generations, the first of which realized they would never live to see the masterpiece completed. Many minute details linger in out-of-the-way corners that the builders knew might never be visible to another human being—only God would see.

The story is told of the hall in an old university with massive oak beams that had undergone centuries of wear and dry rot and now needed to be replaced. Searches were made for hundreds of miles around and no lumber could be found large enough. That is, until the repairmen found original plans for the hall in an old utility closet and realized that the oak trees planted on the grounds when construction of the hall started hundreds of years ago had actually been intended for just such a need.

There were no awards or fanfare for the forethought of the first builders and they weren't alive to see their plan come full circle. Yet it was their intentionality and faithfulness in the labor of building that produced the magnificent trees ready for a time of need.[41]

We easily get bored by too much "sameness" or repetition in our days. G.K. Chesterton posited that this may come from our smallness, rather than our maturity, as we usually imagine. He wrote,

Because children have abounding vitality, because they are in spirit fierce and free, therefore they want things repeated and unchanged. They always say, "Do it again"; and the grown-up person does it again until he is nearly dead. For grown-up

---

41   Story originally drawn from George Grant.

people are not strong enough to exult in monotony. But perhaps God is strong enough to exult in monotony. It is possible that God says every morning, "Do it again" to the sun; and every evening, "Do it again" to the moon. It may not be automatic necessity that makes all daisies alike; it may be that God makes every daisy separately, but has never got tired of making them.[42]

The farmer takes delight in the feel of the soil, the sprouting of seeds and the abundance of a table bursting with a riot of harvest. We are created to rejoice in the small things: the things that come again and again. The season of fresh corn slathered in butter and salt. The season of pumpkin hunts and children begging to sleep by the tree on Christmas Eve. The season of hanging tree swings and watching caterpillars and taking lunch outside. God is glorified by our expectant, eager delight in the world He has made.

Remembering God

The thing to remember in all the hilarity and newly made caramel popcorn burning our fingers and satisfaction of a bonfire on a fall evening is that none of these are actually the point. We can all too easily confuse the gifts and the Giver of all good gifts. We twist His good gifts when we put them on pedestals to be admired by themselves. They are arrows pointing us to Christ, who is the Beginning and End of all things, the One by whom and for whom all things were made; the Word by whom all things came into existence.

No golden, frosty winter morning or breathless, rosy-cheeked child comes to us from anywhere except His hand.

---

42   G.K. Chesterton, *Orthodoxy* (San Francisco, Ignatius Press, 1995), pp. 65, 66.

He is the One who thought up these things and *He* is the One to whom our thoughts should turn in every painful and joyful and ordinary moment. The very things we enjoy in this life should help us understand and exult more deeply in the character of our God. The whiteness of snow is meant to point us to the purity and brilliance of Christ. The life-giving nature of water helps us better understand how Jesus is the One who, as the Water of Life, sustains our life (Ps. 72:6).[43]

It is not that God somehow mimics the things of this life–it's that they were designed to showcase and imitate facets of His character and, in so doing, to put them on display for our slow minds and distracted moments. A million wonderful, good, wholesome things in this life shout for us to see the excellencies of our King. They're like magnifying glasses for our weak eyes to help us better understand what it means that our God is creative and kind and merciful and mighty. We need physical realities to help our spiritual eyes to see properly. That's why, for instance, God has given us the Lord's Supper to sustain our souls in the reality of Christ and His death and resurrection on our behalf.

He knows our weakness and delights to give us the very things we need to understand, to grow, and to delight in Him. He is a good God whose very abundance spills over and drenches us, His creatures. We have the privilege of imitating Him as we give good gifts to our children, filling them up with beautiful, warming, enriching things and surrounding them with that which will point them to the delights of an eternal destiny with One who makes whole everything around Him.

---

43   Joe Rigney, *Strangely Bright* (Crossway, 2020) is an excellent book on this topic.

10

A Compass in the Fog

See, this alone I found, that God made man upright,
but they have sought out many schemes.

ECCLESIASTES 7:29

The days since writing the first chapter of this book have held the birth of our third child, Ryle Asa. Several days after Ryle made his appearance, my knee swelled alarmingly and we spent an afternoon and night in the ER undergoing blood draws, X-rays, ultrasounds, CAT scans, and a six-inch needle drawing fluid from my knee. These tests ruled out a life-threatening blood clot, an infection (which would have led to surgery), and gout, before finally resulting in a diagnosis of Lyme disease.

The swelling finally subsided a few days later, only to give way to the worst stomach bug our house has had in years, which hit the one-year-old at her father's office and in the wee hours of multiple mornings, then our three-year-old on the sidewalk just before entering church *and* in the car on the way home, and all the rest of the adults in our house the next day. We had a week to get back to "normal" life, then my knee swelled up again and we're currently on week six of mommy unable to walk.

"You are good, and what you do is good. Teach me your precepts (Psalm 119:68)," has been a refrain of my heart these past weeks. We all want to learn and grow in the ways of the Lord, but none of us want the days that cause us to learn and to grow the most. Patience and peace wear thin amid days like these and children, of course, pick up on this with increased misbehavior and attitudes that leave much to be desired.

Ana, our almost-two-year-old, is known around here as The One Who Will Find Things Which Ought Not To Be Found and fully lives up to that reputation. Sometime in the past few days, a bag of vitamin bottles was surreptitiously relocated to another room for an opportune time, which was determined to be while mommy was on the phone and daddy was working and there would be adequate opportunity to open at least three of the bottles and sample their contents.

It only took a minute for her to find the door to a forbidden room (which had accidentally been left open) and climb the steep stairs to an attic which is neither safe nor secure. She was found placidly looking out the window and surveying the scene three stories below. Oh, and there was the ten-pound mammoth sweet potato grown by some friends of ours and adopted by our daughters as the resident "baby" to be wrapped in blankets, rocked to sleep, stowed lovingly in the baby seat, and, according to Ana, dumped quickly and skillfully on the head of her newborn brother.

I do hope you're laughing by now, because it's been "either laugh or cry about it" over here for a while now—and we've done both.

Realms of Fog

In a scene from *The Voyage of the Dawn Treader*, the ship enters a realm of thick fog and darkness. The crew of the ship begin to be chilled and disoriented; then, they meet a man who has been trapped there for decades and implores them to escape immediately. It is, in fact, an island where dreams come true— and not the good kind. "They were rowing back to the light as hard as they could," wrote Lewis. "… it would be all right in a few seconds. But oh, if only it could be all right now!"[44]

They rowed and rowed, and some thought they were going in circles:

> *Lucy leant her head on the edge of the fighting-top and whispered, 'Aslan, Aslan, if ever you loved us at all, send us help now.'*
>
> *The darkness did not grow any less, but she began to feel a little—very, very little—better…In a few moments the darkness turned into a greyness ahead, and then, almost before they dared to begin hoping, they had shot out into the sunlight and were in the warm, blue world again. And all at once everybody realized that there was nothing to be afraid of and never had been.[45]*

We all face times like these in our lives in varying degrees of darkness and nightmare. Our past two months have been comparatively trivial. Whether facing a blackness that extends for years, or a slight fog that clears in an afternoon, God asks each of us to trust the wisdom of His providence and the

---

44   C.S. Lewis, *The Voyage of the Dawn Treader* (New York: HarborTrophy, 1980), p. 198.

45   Ibid., pp. 200, 201.

kindness of His guiding hand which brings good and ill alike. As William Cowper, the hymn writer, phrased it:

> *Judge not the Lord by feeble sense,*
> *But trust Him for His grace;*
> *Behind a frowning providence*
> *He hides a smiling face.*

Truths of God's sovereignty and the meaning behind hardship are often learned by our minds on the flourishing pastures of life, but it takes hard rain and storms for them to sink deep in the soil of our hearts and bring forth fruit. Only looking to Christ can bring about real peace in the storms—not idols of comfort, distraction, attention, self-pity, or any others we set up for ourselves.

The Life of Jesus

Words from 2 Corinthians have returned to me once again: "For we who live are always being given over to death for Jesus' sake, so that the life of Jesus also may be manifested in our mortal flesh" (2 Cor. 4:11). These words sound wonderful, and we move on to the next verse. But what does it really mean for "the life of Jesus to be manifested in our mortal flesh"? For me, right now, that seems to mean a trust in the wisdom that has laid me up just when I feel like my family needs me the most. It means restraining irritation at the misbehavior of a toddler who carefully dumps their scrambled eggs on the floor and patiently disciplining them for repeat offenses.

It is my everyday thoughts and words and actions between the hours of 6 a.m. and 10 p.m. that must come under the lordship of Christ and manifest His kindness, gentleness, and love to those around me—even those *most* around me pulling on my sweatshirt ties, leaning on my painful knee, and sticking exploratory fingers into my ear while I'm nursing the baby.

Those around us who have never tasted the sweetness of Christ will think our sacrifices meaningless, our principles too rigid. As Paul puts it so succinctly in 1 Corinthians 15:19, "If in Christ we have hope in this life only, we are of all people most to be pitied." We can slip into cynicism (the hopelessness of an Ecclesiastes without the gospel) if we are not on guard. We get tired. We get lazy. We cannot handle the pressures of our responsibilities. Sometimes, the smaller annoyances can be harder to recognize from His hand than the bigger trials.

When the fog closes in, everything gets a bit darker and it becomes difficult to see the rigging of the ship that surrounds us and to remember the truths we know to be real despite our circumstances. We struggle to remember the point of it all. In these moments, we must fight to believe with all our hearts that *everything* to which Jesus calls us as mothers is good, is for *our* good, and that He equips us with strength for the battle. My mother-in-law often quotes a little-known hymn, "Our Father is too wise to be mistaken…too good to be unkind."[46] It takes tenacious faith to believe this and to cling to it as we walk through this life. Sometimes, this means putting mind over heart, setting our eyes on what we know to be true rather than what feels true in any given moment.

The Loveliness of Christ

Our lives are a massive proving ground for our claim that the gospel is true, that God really did create the world, that Jesus

---

46 Samuel Medley, "God Shall Alone the Refuge Be," public domain.

really did redeem fallen sinners like us, and that He really is returning one day to vindicate the righteous and renew creation. We mothers cannot afford, in our dangerous, world-defeating mission, to grow weary in doing good or to forget the gospel that anchors us. We must find and pursue those things that lead to our peace and lasting joy and cling hard to them each and every morning, every weary evening, and every moment in between.

Many of the sins committed along the way of mothering can seem small and innocent. They seem excusable, given the circumstances and the fact that people on Instagram are probably making memes and laughing about the same things. We can feel rather justified in our sinful actions and attitudes, or even victimized by the neediness of our children, the forgetfulness of our husband, and the general demands placed on us which (we think to ourselves) really are quite too much to bear and make us well deserving of some "me time." Yet it is the very acknowledgement of our sin and guilt and our confession to God and those around us that frees us. Recognizing our sin for what it is frees us to accept the freedom earned by Christ for us on the cross.

God Himself has given us means of dwelling on the loveliness of Christ: the preaching of the Word, prayer, and fellowship with other believers. We cannot afford to neglect these. Instead of guiltily retreating from Christ when we do not want to open our Bibles in the morning, when worship feels like a drag, or when our prayer life feels stale, we can plead with our gentle Shepherd who knows the hardness and frailty of our hearts. We can be honest with Him about the state of our hearts and ask Him to soften us, to enliven us, to make eternal things bright in our sight.

The disciplines of grace woven into the fabric of our days give them steadfastness. We can underestimate the value of the small cracks of time scattered in our days that could be filled with meditation on the Word, hymns, audiobooks, and Scripture read out loud. Even the most ordinary habits—perhaps even *especially* the most ordinary habits—become the liturgy of our homes as we raise up the souls of men and women into eternity.[47]

He who flung the stars into the sky and calls them all by name stands over us to bless us, and the greatest thing He could give us in all the universe is more of Himself. He longs to draw us close. He pleads with us and woos us, even (especially) in our sin. When we fail, we need not be afraid to turn to Him.

Christ alone is the brightness that can break the fog and darkness. Gazing at Him and His loveliness is the only thing that steers our ship through the waves toward the land not of despair but of all the bright hopes and dreams for which we were made. The clearer our vision of Him, the more our hearts burn within us as He illumines the Word of God and plants its truth deep in our hearts. There the air grows clearer, brighter. Psalm 119 is a beacon of light reflecting the radiance and hope that belong to all who trust in Christ. Here is a small sampling of the verses in this rich chapter:

> Remember your word to your servant,
>   in which you have made me hope.

---

47 *Habits of the Household* by Justin Whitmel Earley (Zondervan, 2021) is an excellent book on this topic (though his parenting advice veers a bit into unbiblical "gentle parenting" methods).

This is my comfort in my affliction,
    that your promise gives me life.
v. 49-50

Your statutes have been my songs
    in the house of my sojourning.
I remember your name in the night, O LORD,
    and keep your law.
v. 54-55

It is good for me that I was afflicted,
    that I might learn your statutes.
The law of your mouth is better to me
    than thousands of gold and silver pieces.
v. 71-72

Your hands have made and fashioned me;
    give me understanding that I may learn
    your commandments.
Those who fear you shall see me and rejoice,
    because I have hoped in your word.
I know, O LORD, that your rules are righteous,
    and that in faithfulness you have afflicted me.
Let your steadfast love comfort me
    according to your promise to your servant.
Let your mercy come to me, that I may live;
    for your law is my delight.
v. 73-77

In This, We Are Filled

The eyes of faith fix their gaze on what God has promised in His Word, despite influences on our heart or emotions to the contrary. As we steam green beans out of a desire to faithfully serve the Lord and mediate between forever squabbling siblings, fighting the good fight against building resentment, we glorify the Lord. In Christ, God is pleased with us, despite our stumbling efforts.

We are given the graces of these daily tasks and habits to remind the discouraged among us that He grants new morning mercies with strength and identity for each day; and to remind the proud among us that it is *He* who grants us these things. We receive from Him our time and toast and plates and clothes and the energy to accomplish our work.

As we nourish bellies, the Lord Himself fills our souls and as we lay down our time for yet another sink of dishes, our kind Father multiplies the efforts of our soapy hands to build something lasting in us and in the lives of our families. As we sacrifice in the daily work of motherhood, we are becoming living sacrifices ourselves, relying on Christ, the ultimate Sacrifice, for the grace to be grace-full and not full of our own strivings or the memories of our own failures.

When Christ Himself returns to claim His bride, all the effects of sin will be wiped away from this hurting world. All our sin, all sin against us, all our struggles, all our joys will pale in comparison as the true Desire of our souls is revealed in the ruling and reigning Lord of all the earth. All the things we laid on the altar and counted as loss for His sake will seem trivial.

One day, the Kingdom will come in its fullness and all the frailty of our bodies and minds will be redeemed for eternity.

"For now we see in a mirror dimly, but then face to face. Now I know in part; then I shall know fully, even as I have been fully known (1 Cor. 13:12)." We'll one day wish our faith had been more steadfast, our feeble efforts more consistent, our obedience more joyful. All the things that once seemed such sacrifices to us will seem small on that side of glory.

Time will be lost into eternity and forever we will praise Him. No longer will we strain against feelings of mundanity, for the glories of what He was working all along despite the curse will be revealed. Our trust and obedience of Him will be seen for what it truly was: confidence in the living and glorious God. Our trading of hot coffee and beautiful silence and clean floors for the winning of hearts in our humble homes will be received by our King as worship, and His name will ring out for all eternity.

> And I heard a loud voice from the throne saying, "Behold, the dwelling place of God is with man. He will dwell with them, and they will be his people, and God himself will be with them as their God. He will wipe away every tear from their eyes, and death shall be no more, neither shall there be mourning, nor crying, nor pain anymore, for the former things have passed away."
>
> And he who was seated on the throne said, "Behold, I am making all things new."
> — Revelation 21:3-5a

Study Questions

Chapter 1: An Introduction

READ ECCLESIASTES 1–2

- Are there difficult aspects of your life which you resent?

- What is revealed in your life by resentment or frustration?

- How does idolatry manifest itself in your life right now?

- In what ways can you confront this sin and rely on the Lord's strength to forsake it?

Chapter 2: Experience and Ecclesiastes

READ HEBREWS 5

- What experiences in life did you feel prepared for until you were in the middle of them?

- Does it change your view of Jesus' relationship with you to realize He has also walked through the sadness, sickness, and death of a fallen world?

- How can you imitate Jesus in your fight against sin, self, and worldliness?

Chapter 3: All Is Vanity—or Is It?

READ PSALM 34 AND PSALM 103

- List a few biblical truths about your life that give you hope. How can you actively cling to those realities in the middle of busy days?

- What verses speak to difficult realities you are facing? Write them out and post them in your bathroom, kitchen, or office where you can see them often and meditate on them.

- Does it feel strange that all you bring to God is need?

- What are things you subconsciously feel like you bring to the table of grace? What does this reveal about your heart?

Chapter 4: Remembering the Goal

READ PHILIPPIANS 2:1-18

- How do situations in which you fail or come up short make you feel? What is true of you in Christ even in the middle of these situations (not just after you've repented)?

- What does it mean to confront and hate your sin, while also realizing that God uses it to accomplish His purposes in your life?

- What parts of parenthood or homemaking are the hardest for you right now? Pray and work to remember that you are doing *that* particular thing out of love for Jesus today.

- Does it change your view of hard things to realize God uses these to accomplish the most in your journey of sanctification?

Chapter 5: Who Is Sufficient?

READ 2 CORINTHIANS 2:14-5:21

- Are you comfortable when others see your weaknesses? What areas of weakness have you been given right now?

- How is God teaching you to rely on His strength in these areas?

- How can you speak to others about the power of God that He has manifested in these particular areas of your life? If that is uncomfortable for you, think about what might be causing that. Might your hesitancy to speak of God's faithfulness need to be confessed as an area of sin?

Chapter 6: Motherhood as Suffering

READ PHILIPPIANS 2:1-11

- What things have you thought you would love to do to serve the Lord that He has not called you to? What areas of your calling do you dislike or struggle in right now?

- What experiences, goals, or recognition once seemed all-important to you but now seem insignificant? What about a passing comment or conversation that seemed small in the moment but still impacts you years later?

Pray that God would give you wisdom to distinguish between the trivial and the eternal in your parenting and relationships each day.

- Does it change your view of mothering to see it (in part) as suffering? How does God promise to help the suffering and the weak?

Chapter 7: Hope in Childbearing

READ ECCLESIASTES 11

- List a few things that come quickly and leave quickly (i.e. a cup of coffee, cut flowers, a movie). List a few things that took years, decades, or centuries, but will endure for much longer (i.e. a cathedral, a tree, a quilt). What things are you making, building, or growing right now that you hope will outlive you?

- Would it change your life to live intentionally for the next ten years? Are there things you might choose to do differently?

- How do temporary things you do point to lasting things?

- How are you teaching your children to value lasting things (physically and spiritually)?

Chapter 8: The Apologetic of Motherhood

READ 1 CORINTHIANS 15

- What does it mean to preach the gospel to yourself?

- What areas of laying down your life in motherhood are easier for you? What aspects are harder? How can Christ's example of laying down His life encourage you?

- How would you describe the difference between sanctification and justification? What do the realities of justification mean for your daily life? What about sanctification?

- What does it mean for our parenting to see our children as eternal souls? How does it change our priorities to see those around us as eternal souls?

Chapter 9: The Magic of Simple

READ PSALM 72

- Do you tend toward laziness or obsessive order? How can you cultivate both intention and extravagance as you reflect God in your homemaking?

- Make a list of simple, everyday ways you can build a celebratory atmosphere into the life of your home.

- How does it change your view of the good things in your life to see them as specifically designed to show you more of your God?

Chapter 10: A Compass in the Fog

READ PSALM 119:49-80

- During what times in your life has it been hard to remember truth because of the "fog" around you?

- How have you learned more about God through seasons of suffering?

- In what ways have you become more like Christ because of hardship?

- How have others comforted you in ways that enabled you to look to Christ rather than becoming self-focused or indulging in self-pity?

- What small sins do you indulge in because they are excused or endearingly caricatured by the culture? What are the biblical names for these sins (e.g. to be "stressed" is to be anxious)? What does the Bible say about that specific sin?

- How can you remind yourself of eternal hope each day?

Also available from Christian Focus Publications ...

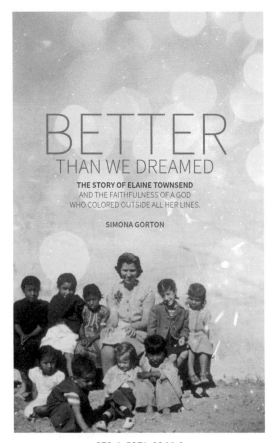

BETTER
THAN WE DREAMED

THE STORY OF ELAINE TOWNSEND
AND THE FAITHFULNESS OF A GOD
WHO COLORED OUTSIDE ALL HER LINES.

SIMONA GORTON

978-1-5271-0266-8

Better Than We Dreamed
The Story of Elaine Townsend
by Simona Gorton

Read the story of a life lived safely within the lines, that God turned upside down. From social star of 1930's Chicago to a Wycliffe missionary in South America and the USSR, Elaine Townsend's life was far from boring. Meet the woman who became Cameron Townsend's wife, and discover how a life can be filled with adventure, by simply saying 'yes' to God.

Through each stage of Elaine's life her trust and dependence on her Saviour shines as an example to believers everywhere, yet there are also weaknesses with which we can all identify. This account of her struggles and successes is filled with stories gathered from those who knew Elaine best, as well as insights into the mission work that renewed a generation's passion for Bible translation.

Both encouraging and challenging, this thorough biography leads the reader to rightly recognise Elaine Townsend as one of the great Christian women of the 20th century – a demonstration of what God can do with a willing heart.

This delightfully written and meticulously researched narrative traces her footsteps around the globe, recalling her life of devotion to Cameron and her indefatigable zeal in proclaiming the mission of God to the world. May her earnestness and joy be an encouragement to all.

STEPHEN J. NICHOLS
President, Reformation Bible College
Sanford, Florida

10
WOMEN
WHO
WERE
SPIRITUAL
MOTHERS

Dayspring
MacLeod

978-1-5271-0972-8

10 Women Who Were Spiritual Mothers

by Dayspring MacLeod

Motherhood. Not for the faint hearted or blasé, it's a state of being that tries one's patience, purpose and peace.

In tackling themes from purity to patience, each focused narrative allows the reader an insight into the lives of women whom they may have heard of but not known well. From Katherine Parr, sixth and final wife of Henry VIII, to Sharon Dickens and Lisa Harper, the ten women represent a spectrum of life delivered via the prism of motherhood.

This book isn't only for mothers. It's for those who are heartbroken, single, bereft or at peace in later life. Discipleship is a key theme, be it with the children who litter your hallways with Nerf Pellets or friends undergoing the ups and downs of infertility. As a woman who knows the support of women in her own life, Macleod has gracefully painted a canvas of joy in sorrows, peace and panic and Christ's love triumphant.

This is not a book for the faint-hearted but neither is motherhood in any of its forms. Time spent on this serious study of motherhood will bear fruit in families and church families. To God be the glory!

IRENE HOWAT
Award-winning author

IDOLS
of a
MOTHER'S
HEART

CHRISTINA FOX

978-1-5271-0233-0

Idols of a Mother's Heart
by Christina Fox

Even good things can become idols if we give them central importance in our lives. Having children changes everything, and as mothers, we risk looking for life, purpose and meaning in motherhood. While being a mother brings its unique set of challenges, these years of raising children and helping them grow in the nurture and admonition of the Lord provide an opportunity to grow in our own Christlikeness as well.

Writing from her own personal experience as a mom, Christina Fox encourages mothers to prayerfully and thoughtfully examine their own hearts, and to let God use motherhood as a means of sanctification.

Split into three sections, the first chapter looks at the meaning motherhood; chapters 2–4 are about idolatry; chapters 5–9 focus on a few different idols that mothers might worship (not an exhaustive list, but a common few); and the final chapters are about facing idols, dethroning them, and turning our heart back to the One true God.

With penetrating questions, humble honesty, and gospel freedom on every page, this book will not only stretch and challenge a mother, but point her to the joy and satisfaction found in her Savior alone.

LAURA WIFLER
Co–Founder of Risen Motherhood

Christian Focus Publications

Our mission statement

Staying Faithful

In dependence upon God we seek to impact the world through literature faithful to His infallible Word, the Bible. Our aim is to ensure that the Lord Jesus Christ is presented as the only hope to obtain forgiveness of sin, live a useful life and look forward to heaven with Him.

Our Books are published in four imprints:

⟨◯✕ CHRISTIAN FOCUS

Popular works including biographies, commentaries, basic doctrine and Christian living.

⟨◯✕ MENTOR

Books written at a level suitable for Bible College and seminary students, pastors, and other serious readers. The imprint includes commentaries, doctrinal studies, examination of current issues and church history.

⟨◯✕ CHRISTIAN HERITAGE

Books representing some of the best material from the rich heritage of the church.

⟨◯✕ CF4KIDS

Children's books for quality Bible teaching and for all age groups: Sunday school curriculum, puzzle and activity books; personal and family devotional titles, biographies and inspirational stories – because you are never too young to know Jesus!

Christian Focus Publications Ltd,
Geanies House, Fearn, Ross-shire,
IV20 1TW, Scotland, United Kingdom.
www.christianfocus.com